MW01009743

Palgrave Studies in Workplace Spirituality and Fulfillment

Series Editors
Satinder Dhiman
School of Business
Woodbury University
Burbank, CA, USA

Gary Roberts
Regent University
Virginia Beach, VA, USA

Joanna Crossman
University of South Australia
Adelaide, SA, Australia

Satinder Dhiman
Editor-in-Chief

Gary Roberts and Joanna Crossman
Associate Editors

By way of primary go-to-platform, this Series precisely maps the terrain of the twin fields of *Workplace Spirituality and Fulfillment* in the disciplines of business, psychology, health care, education, and various other allied fields. It reclaims the sacredness of work—work that is mind-enriching, heart-fulfilling, soul-satisfying and financially-rewarding. It fills the gap in scholarship in the allied disciplines of Workplace Spirituality and Flourishing. Using a comprehensive schema, it invites contributions from foremost scholars and practitioners that reflect insightful research, practices, and latest trends on the theme of workplace spirituality and fulfillment. The uniqueness of this *Series* lies in its anchorage in the moral and spiritual dimension of various positive forms of leadership—such as Authentic Leadership, Servant Leadership, Transformational Leadership, and Values-Based Leadership.

We welcome research monographs and multi-authored edited volumes representing myriad thought-positions on topics such as: Past, Present and Future Directions in Workplace Spirituality; Workplace Spirituality and World Wisdom/Spiritual Traditions; Culture Studies and Workplace Spirituality; Spiritual, Social and Emotional intelligence; Nature of Work; Mindfulness at Work; Personal Fulfillment and Workplace Flourishing; Workplace Spirituality and Organizational Performance; Inner Identity, Interconnectedness, Community and Transcendence; Managing Spiritual and Religious Diversity at Work; Spirituality and World Peace Imperative; Sustainability and Spirituality; Spirituality and Creativity; and Applied Workplace Spirituality in Health Care, Education, Faith-based Organizations, et al.

More information about this series at
http://www.palgrave.com/gp/series/15746

John Henry Horsman

Servant-Leaders in Training

Foundations of the Philosophy of Servant-Leadership

Foreword by Larry C. Spears

palgrave
macmillan

John Henry Horsman
Gonzaga University
Spokane, WA, USA

Palgrave Studies in Workplace Spirituality and Fulfillment
ISBN 978-3-319-92960-6   ISBN 978-3-319-92961-3   (eBook)
https://doi.org/10.1007/978-3-319-92961-3

Library of Congress Control Number: 2018948852

This Palgrave Macmillan imprint is published by the registered company Springer Nature Switzerland AG
The registered company address is: Gewerbestrasse 11, 6330 Cham, Switzerland

Foreword

I am honored to write the foreword to *Servant-Leaders in Training: Foundations of the Philosophy of Servant-Leadership*. Let me tell you why.

I was first introduced to the servant-as-leader idea in 1982. At that time, I was working with *Friends Journal*, a Quaker magazine based in Philadelphia. We received an article submission from Robert K. Greenleaf on the servant-as-leader idea, which we eventually published. All these years later, I still recall the "a-ha" moment that came over me as I read Greenleaf's description of servant-leadership. I found that he had given a name to an undefined yearning that I felt within me. I knew that I wanted to do what I could to help make the world a little better place in which to live. I was doing what I could to be of service in that goal, and I hoped that I might eventually have an opportunity to provide some leadership. In reading Greenleaf's definition and best test of a servant-as-leader, I began to understand servant-leadership as a personal philosophy that could be developed and practiced. All these years later, I continue in my personal and public efforts to practice servant-leadership. My reading and re-reading of John Horsman's *Servant-leaders in Training: Foundations of the Philosophy of Servant-Leadership* has proven to be so helpful in my continuing inquiry into servant-leadership, for which I am most grateful.

I first met John Horsman in 2005, when he participated in a program called the Leadership Institute for Higher Education (LIFE), sponsored by the Robert K. Greenleaf Center, and where I was privileged to serve as

President and CEO from 1990 to 2007. In 1990, I had a chance to spend time with Robert Greenleaf, and I eventually edited or co-edited all five of Robert Greenleaf's available books, as well as a series of popular servant-leadership anthologies. In 2008, I started a new phase of my work in servant-leadership when I was invited to serve as Servant-Leadership Scholar for Gonzaga University. That same year, I also launched the Spears Center for Servant-Leadership, and thus, I began to divide my time between these two institutions, which I continue to do.

While I have had a long history as a writer and editor of books on servant-leadership, in 2008 I was a complete novice when it came to teaching graduate courses in servant-leadership. Thankfully, I was blessed to have the wonderful guidance and support of several of my faculty colleagues at Gonzaga—including John Horsman—who helped to orient me to teaching servant-leadership within the construct of graduate courses.

Over the years, John and I have spent considerable time collaborating and teaching two graduate courses at Gonzaga University: Servant-Leadership and Listen, Discern, Decide. Both courses are deeply grounded in Robert K. Greenleaf's fundamental understanding of what it means to be a servant-leader. John is a consummate teacher, and I have learned much from him. Thanks to John, I have come to discover that my own calling in servant-leadership joyfully encompasses the role of teaching. John's many years of experience as a servant-leader teacher has contributed greatly to the powerful ideas contained within this book.

Robert Greenleaf was 73 years old when he published his first book, *Servant-Leadership*. Much like Robert Greenleaf before him, John has waited a long time until he was ready to publish this, his first book. Also like Greenleaf, John has spent many years practicing and teaching servant-leadership, leading up to the distillation of his thoughts here. In truth, I believe that *Foundations of the Philosophy of Servant-Leadership* is one of the most important books to be published in this field since Robert Greenleaf first published *Servant-Leadership*.

Who *is* a servant-leader? Greenleaf said that the servant-leader is one who is a servant first. In *The Servant as Leader* he wrote, "It begins with the natural feeling that one wants to serve, to serve first. Then conscious choice brings one to aspire to lead. The difference manifests itself in the care taken by the servant—first to make sure that other people's highest priority needs are being served. The best test is: Do those served grow as persons; do they, while being served, become healthier, wiser, freer, more autonomous, more likely themselves to become servants? And, what is the effect on the least privileged in society? Will they benefit or at least not be further deprived?"

It is important to remember that servant-leadership begins within every one of us. As a lifelong student of how things get done in organizations, Greenleaf distilled his observations in a series of essays and books on the theme of "The Servant as Leader"—the objective of which was to stimulate thought and action for building a better, more caring society.

The servant-leader concept continues to grow in its influence and impact. In fact, we have witnessed a remarkable growth of awareness and practices of servant-leadership. In many ways, it may be said that the times are only now beginning to catch up with Robert Greenleaf's visionary call to servant-leadership. The idea of servant-leadership, now in its fifth decade as a concept bearing that name, continues to create a quiet revolution around the world.

The words servant and leader are usually thought of as being opposites. In deliberately bringing those two words together in a meaningful way, Robert Greenleaf gave birth to the paradoxical term "servant-leader." In the years since then, many of today's most creative thinkers are writing and speaking about servant-leadership as an emerging paradigm for the twenty-first century. Robert Greenleaf's writings on the subject of servant-leadership helped to get this movement started, and his views have had a profound and growing effect on many organizations and thought-leaders. Organizations like Starbucks, TDIndustries, The Toro Company, Southwest Airlines, The Men's Wearhouse, Synovus Financial Corporation, The Container Store, and many more are recognized today for nurturing servant-led cultures. These and many more organizational practitioners have been encouraged and supported by a long list of thought-leaders such as James Autry, Warren Bennis, Ken Blanchard, Peter Block, John Carver, Stephen Covey, Max DePree, Shann Ferch, Don Frick, Joseph Jaworski, James Kouzes, Larraine Matusak, Parker Palmer, M. Scott Peck, Peter Senge, Peter Vaill, Margaret Wheatley, and Danah Zohar, to name but a handful of today's cutting-edge authors and advocates of servant-leadership. With *Foundations of the Philosophy of Servant-Leadership*, we add John

Horsman to this list of seminal thought-leaders who are helping to shape our ongoing understanding of servant-leadership.

In 1992, I conducted a study of Robert Greenleaf's writings. From that analysis, I was able to codify a set of ten characteristics that Greenleaf wrote about and which he considered as being central to the development of servant-leaders. These include listening, empathy, healing, awareness, persuasion, conceptualization, foresight, stewardship, commitment to the growth of people, and building community. These ten characteristics of servant-leadership are by no means exhaustive. However, they serve to communicate the power and promise that this concept offers to servant-leaders who are open to its invitation and challenge. In *Foundations of the Philosophy of Servant-Leadership*, John Horsman offers a more complete understanding of listening, foresight, and other characteristics associated with servant-leadership.

Becoming a servant-leader in training is a personal development process. As John writes, it is "a process that enhances our awareness, our authenticity, and our integrity and in turn our relational capacity to respond to others. A servant-consciousness involves building on all that we have learned up to this point in time." Likewise, his emphasis on dispositions and capacities of servant-leaders significantly helps to move forward our understanding of what it means to be a servant-leader.

In *Servant-leaders in Training: Foundations of the Philosophy of Servant-Leadership*, John guides us through the deep current of servant-leadership as a philosophy. His focus on human development, personal relationships, creativity, human integration, moral authority, servant-consciousness, listening, and foresight provides an important breakthrough in our contemporary understanding of servant-leadership.

In our servant-leadership courses at Gonzaga University, we are fond of using the phrase, "servant-leader in training." This serves as a reminder that all of us are, always, Servant-leaders in training. And while there are no perfect servant-leaders, through our ongoing development and practice, we can become *authentic* servant-leaders.

I would like to add that one of the unexpected delights of this book is to be found in the charts and figures that John has included throughout this volume. These charts capture the essence of great theories of human development and help to make them understandable in their relevance to the servant-leadership philosophy.

I invite you to read what is contained within this book and to consider becoming a servant-leader in training—one who serves first and then looks for opportunities to lead. Here, John Horsman has managed to take servant-leadership and to expand upon it, making it more inclusive, more holistic, and more integrated than ever before. Through his examination of the servant-leadership philosophy, Horsman also reminds us that servant-leadership begins within every one of us.

Servant-Leadership Scholar, Gonzaga University   Larry C. Spears

Senior Advisory Editor, *The International Journal of Servant-Leadership*

President, The Spears Center for Servant-Leadership, Inc.

Editor, *Insights on Leadership* Indianapolis, IN, USA

Preface

I find it fascinating that Robert K. Greenleaf published his first writings on Servant-leading at the cutting edge of leadership history (1970s), when *leadership* began emerging as a distinct academic school of thought. In the historically short time since, the subject matter of Servant-leadership has intrigued and perplexed academics and practitioners while continuing to gain a foothold as an emerging leadership philosophy. What is most captivating about the desire to *serve-first* is that it profoundly clarifies and contextualizes a motive, a purpose, and a way to lead. Servant-leading calls for a grander, more inclusive, more naturally human, and a more interdependent approach to leading than all the variations of self-serving and power-oriented leadership. What is most perplexing about Servant-leadership is that mastery eludes us.

Much of what Robert K. Greenleaf wrote on Servant-leading was prophetic, and a flow of significant new meaning has continued to emerge from my years of studying, teaching, and designing graduate courses based on Greenleaf's thinking. What I have learned is that desiring to *serve-first* is an ancient, current, and future way to lead and will continue to capture our imagination and yearning for true leadership. Nevertheless, despite all the qualitative and quantitative research on the topic, all of which has expanded and deepened our understanding, it remains difficult to put a circle around Servant-leadership and say *this is what it is*—there always seems to be more to it. Servant-leadership as articulated by Greenleaf seems to resist precise and satisfactory categorization and operationalization. Indeed, the more we learn and practice Servant-leading, the more it remains before us like a mystery calling us forth to greater creative depths of awareness, understanding, and practice. This is why I am convinced Servant-leadership continues to be an emerging philosophy.

The emerging philosophy of Servant-leadership is a framework which is becoming an attractor for many complementary best practices. Today, many great organizational and system best practices seem to be drifting around like individuated fragments with no philosophical anchoring. The philosophy of Servant-leadership is inherently inclusive of procedures and practices that adhere to the values and skills that nurture profoundly relational, creative, holistic, and integrative human flourishing.

This writing is not a book of stories or examples, nor is it a summation of recent research, it is a distillation of many stories and some research for the purpose of expanding on what is known and evolving the philosophy of Servant-leadership. Similarly to Greenleaf, what is proposed herein is descriptive and directional, rather than definitive. The primary focus of this writing is to take Greenleaf's thinking a little further, not to complete it, rather, in a similar theme to Greenleaf's original approach, to creatively attempt to make the vision a little more whole and a little more integrative and, in doing so, add some clarity and perhaps some greater complexity. What is presented here does not intend to dilute the characteristics of Servant-leaders identified from Greenleaf's writings; it underscores and extends, expands, and deepens their importance. This writing assumes the reader is familiar with Greenleaf's writings on Servant-leading or that Greenleaf's writing and edited works are being read as complements to this exposition.

As a teacher of graduate students in organizational leadership, the natural audience for this writing is practitioner scholars, leaders, and emerging leaders. Students are great teachers, I have learned much from many women and men who became willing to embrace the subject matter as *Servant-leaders in training*, and our mutual insights are embedded in this work. Moreover, I extend my humble appreciation to Larry Spears, a colleague and friend, whose scholarly writing and editing and teaching are synonymous with Greenleaf's work and who has done much to further our collective conceptualization of Servant-leading.

The book is specifically focused on the latter two stages of human development, stages that have not been well addressed within Servant-leadership to date. Several relevant human development models are drawn from to show that we are all potentially on a developmental journey, and our leadership is a mirror as well as a forum for learning about the journey. The overview of human development provides a very usable framework for understanding leadership, training, and development. The developmental framework sets the direction and identifies the values and skills required for leadership training and development. The outcome is a more comprehensive, holistic, and integrated justification for the future practice and study of Servant-leadership.

Greenleaf's ideas guide the topic development throughout the book. The journey begins with the introduction of the galaxy symbol and some concepts that seem to be natural additions to Greenleaf's philosophy. The first chapter introduces and addresses assumptions and barriers and explores the motivations and resistance within the philosophy that are helpful for beginning the journey. Chapters 2 and 3 present human development as a framework for understanding leader and organizational development. A skeletal framework of human development maps four successive developmental stages with corresponding leader typologies. Chapter 4 introduces some new concepts related to Servant-leader development and elaborates on the empathetic moral capacity that is the basis for serving-first and the formation of a profoundly relational disposition. Promoting community becomes more compelling when Servant-leaders embrace the notion of independence–interdependence, a concept introduced as a dynamic, and a symbol, for integrating self-actualization with collective actualization. Chapter 5 addresses interior and exterior listening and introduces the notion of holistic listening, discernment, and influential persuasion. Chapter 6 builds on holistic listening, creativity, aware healing and creative learning, and presencing as integral aspects of pathfinding-foresight. Chapter 7 introduces humility, holism, and wisdom and suggests intentionally attending to our relational responsibilities may build capacity for the development of a servant-consciousness.

Spokane, WA, USA   John Henry Horsman

Contents

List of Figures

List of Tables

1

Profoundly Relational, Creative, Holistic, and Integrative

For a very long time humans have been peering into the universe, as if trying to find or recognize our home, or our way home. Since the time of the last renaissance, we have located our place in our solar system, and in our galaxy, and we have begun searching and probing deeper into the cosmos. As we explore and discover more about our exterior space, we are simultaneously exploring and discovering (bringing into consciousness) more of the infinite interior depths within ourselves. As with any exploration of new territory, we humans find it helpful in the early part of the exploration to first map what we know. The more we map the universe, the more intriguing it becomes, and we always find there is much more to discover. As we have learned to map the structure of space, our perspective and our consciousness of our place in space and our relationship with space evolve.

Somewhat similarly to our experience of probing interior and exterior space, the study of Servant-leading also reveals an expanding perspective that includes much about our interior relationship with ourselves as well as our exterior relationships with others, groups, organizations, communities, and the entire human and ecological global system. Similar to our efforts to map the structures of space to discover and locate where we

© The Author(s) 2018
J. H. Horsman, *Servant-Leaders in Training*,
Palgrave Studies in Workplace Spirituality and Fulfillment,
https://doi.org/10.1007/978-3-319-92961-3_1

are—and where we are not—it is helpful to use the structures of human development to map and evolve a leadership philosophy. Fortunately, multiple models of human development have already been developed, well tested, and found to be quite structurally consistent. The models show the potential for individual development, as well as the historical evolution and development of groups, culture, organizations, and systems. The value of using these human development maps is that we find it quite easy to find where we are currently located on the development journey, and it is also quite easy to locate the people we work with, our group, our organization, and our society. In addition to showing us where we are presently located, the developmental models show us where we have been, and potentially where we might go from here—if we should choose to do so. Models of human development are pertinent frameworks with which to begin explaining the philosophy of Servant-leadership because we can trace the development of leader typologies within the models.

Like peering into the universe, coming to understand Servant-leadership also expands our perspective and, in so doing, serves to nurture the development of an emerging servant-consciousness. A seemingly appropriate iconic symbol for a servant-consciousness is a galaxy spiral. Our Milky Way galaxy, for example, provides us with an expansive view of our place in the universe; it locates our solar system, and our earth home within it. A galaxy spiral is symbolic of a cosmic worldview, a relatively stable worldview that is connected to everything we know even though it is continuously transforming. A cosmic worldview is more expansive than any previous worldviews held in common by humans. A cosmic worldview is an open evolving system, as is a servant-consciousness. A servant-consciousness and a spiraling galaxy can be described as a relatively stable open system in perpetual transformation. Likewise Servant-leadership as perceived and presented herein is a relatively stable open philosophy in perpetual transformation.

Although we may prefer it otherwise, we humans are not evolving toward a more simplified view of the world, or to the way it used to be, we are evolving toward a more complex integrative cosmic worldview—a new worldview that calls for Servant-leaders, who in turn will aide our efforts to better perceive ourselves and our purpose on earth and in the universe. As we enter into the next renaissance, our call is no longer to greater independence, our call now is to independence–interdependence, a dynamic that awakens a more integrated relational awareness within ourselves, with others, with the collective, and with all of creation.

Those who probe the meaning and relevance of Servant-leadership tend to enhance their depth of perception, expand their views, and to some extent become prophetic. Robert K. Greenleaf linked seeking and pro-phetic vision to the task of becoming a Servant-leader. To that end I have also become a seeker, and this work is some of what I have perceived and discovered in my listening and foreseeing. Perhaps some of it will resonate with your own seeking, and we might journey together for a while.

The primary focus of this writing is to take Greenleaf's thinking a little further, not to complete it; rather, in a similar theme to Greenleaf's original approach, to creatively attempt to make the vision a little more whole and a little more integrative, and in doing so add some clarity and perhaps greater complexity to the philosophy of Servant-leadership.

The objective is to further develop Greenleaf's key insights, affirm Servant-leader development within the human development models, and introduce some new conceptual structures to prepare the way for a more comprehensive Servant-leader philosophy. For this purpose, I use the terms Servant-leader and Servant-leadership interchangeably, as in being and doing, with the former reflecting the individual leader and the latter reflecting an individual's interaction with the collective. Servant-leadership is presented herein as an expanding philosophical framework for individual and organizational development. Servant-leadership is offered as a philosophy we can aspire to in our era, and it is a philosophy that will serve us in the age we are entering into. Our purpose entails clarifying the framework of the philosophy and then expanding the phi-losophy by increasing the breadth and depth of our understandings of Servant-leading. The framework is based on values and skills that nurture the development of the person and the organization for the purpose of creating a more caring serving society. As a profoundly relational and moral approach, serving-first potentially nurtures greater meaning and fulfillment, greater relational engagement, and overall greater personal and collective human flourishing.

Expanding the philosophy involves learning and nurturing a more profoundly relational, creative, holistic, and integrated way of being and doing our work in the world. A servant-consciousness arises from serving-first, is inherently transforming, and is inspired by compassion, generosity, gratitude, and joy. A servant-consciousness is harmonious with the associated values and skills that range through the higher stages of human development. The actualization of a servant-consciousness requires a deliberate and creative transforming approach for ourselves and for the people and the collectives within which we interact; it involves nurturing and expanding our capacity for a cosmic worldview. The assumption here is that a servant-consciousness is evolving throughout humankind. Such an approach involves much more than merely coming to understand the philosophy of Servant-leadership; rather, it involves engaging the challenge of becoming a *Servant-leader in training* through practicing, enriching, and clarifying our notions of who we are, our life purposes, and the meaning we derive from pursuing our life quest.

A primary assumption of the human development models is that humans have the capacity to sequentially develop more complex and integrated worldviews along with the values and skills to enable flourishing within those worldviews. Within the models paradigmatic growth is described and categorized. Several of the developmental models reveal leader typologies that emerge within the developmental stages. If the structure of these human development models are accurate, and an enormous amount of research suggests they are, organizations of the future will naturally come to embrace Servant-leadership.

The approach is grounded first in the historical writings of Robert K. Greenleaf; second, in the structural framework (models) of human development and leadership; third, on personal insights from theory and practice teaching Servant-leadership; fourth, on the collective intelligence that has emerged from many researchers, students, and practitioners of Servant-leadership. Regarding the models, Wilber's (2001) *Philosophy of Everything* and his (2006) four-quadrant model that reflects personal consciousness development (I), brain and organizational development (It), culture and worldviews (We), and human systems development (Its) are the foundational reference (see Fig. 1.1). Table 1.1 shows Servant-leader

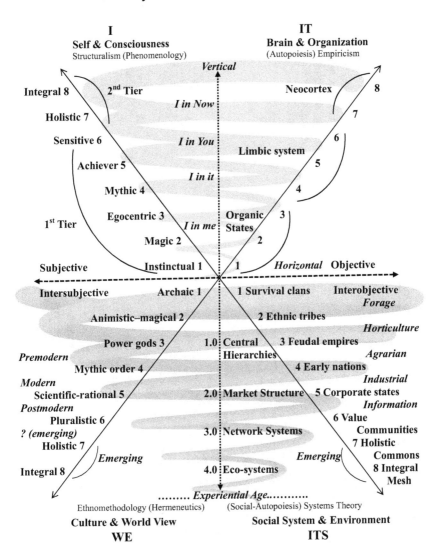

Fig. 1.1 Individual consciousness and collective development. (Adapted from Wilber (2006) *Integral Methodological Pluralism* & Scharmer and Kaufer's (2013) *Learning from the emerging future.*) Printed with permission of Gonzaga University

Table 1.1 Servant-leader development

Developmental Servant-leader values and skills, capacities, disposition, and consciousness			
Values and skills: Servant-leaders	Capacities	Disposition	Consciousness
• Seek awareness, integrity, and humility • Serve with respect and compassion (Greenleaf's test of Servant leadership) • Accept and delegate responsibility • Seek justice and forgiveness	Servant-leaders model an empathetic moral capacity	A Servant-leader disposition is profoundly relational, creative, holistic, and integrative	A *Servant-consciousness* arises from serving-first, is inherently transforming, and is inspired by compassion, generosity, gratitude, and joy
• Promote integrative holism via individual and collective actualizations • Practice independence–interdependence • Promote appreciation, belonging, commitment, confidence, and dependability • Promote congruence, harmony, and trust	Servant-leaders promote community		
• Seek information, knowledge and wisdom • Practice empathetic and generative listening • Practice discernment and generative dialog • Practice influential persuasion	Servant-leaders listens-first seeking clarity before influence		
• Practice presencing • Practice aware healing and creative learning • Envision, conceptualize, enact • Use an adaptive holistic framework	Servant-leaders practice pathfinding-foresight		
• Practice servant-stewardship • Seek whole system synergies • Think and act strategically • Integrate micro, meso, macro, mundo systems	Servant-leaders practice systems thinking		

development based on the development of values and skill, primary capacities, and dispositions culminating in a servant-consciousness.

Brian Hall's (1994) *Value Development* is also broadly drawn on to present human and organizational development based on an understanding of values and skills development to show the development of leader typologies. Additional information is integrated from Beck and Cowan's (1996) *Spiral Dynamics*, Kegan and Lahey's (2009) *Immunity to Change*, and Torbert and Fisher's *Developmental Model of Work and Leadership* (in Thompson, 2000). Information from these developmental models are integrated to provide a synthesized overview of leadership development. As with any eclectic view, what is presented may not be exactly true for any one model, rather what is presented represents a general view based on the writers' view of the whole.

Examples of Servant-leaders can be found throughout history and within every stage of human development; however, as each stage evolves into a more complex and increasingly more socio-centric worldview, Servant-leadership comes into greater and greater fruition. This writing explicitly focuses on the latter two stages of development because these are the focus stages that are still emerging, and the stages with the highest future potential for all of humanity. Generally what habituates us in a particular stage of development, at a particular time, is our perception of the world, awareness of the needs we are striving for, and our perception of how well we are functioning, all of which involves learning, practicing, and integrating relevant values and skills. An implication of the human drive to evolve our awareness stimulates transforming capacities within ourselves and our leadership, all of which nurtures and evolves what I call a servant-consciousness.

Figure 1.1 portraits I and It (upper individual spiral growth) representing eight potential levels of individual subjective objective development beginning from birth. We and Its (lower collective spiral) represent collective historical learning and development through eight potential levels of intersubjective interobjective worldviews and social systems development.

Table 1.1 shows Servant-leader development progressing from influential values and skill development. Each of the five capacities is shown as being supported by sets of four values and related skills; this is not an exclusive list. Spears' (1995) ten characteristics and Sipe and Frick's (2009) pillars of Servant-leadership, and more, are embedded in the capacities, values, and skills.

On Robert Greenleaf

It begins with the natural feeling that one wants to serve, to serve first. Then conscious choice brings one to aspire to lead. (Greenleaf, 1977, p. 13)

The writings of Robert K. Greenleaf (1904–1990) are seminal to understanding Servant-leadership. Greenleaf offered much sage advice and described a number of Servant-leader capacities. He also prescribed how we might become Servant-leaders and offered the best test for Servant-leadership. Greenleaf's first essay, *Servant as Leader* (1970), was initially embraced by a number of individual practitioners and innovative groups; however, the two successive essays *Institution as Servant* (1972) and *Trustees as Servant* (1972) were resisted and largely dismissed by many corporate leaders—at the time. Having spent 38 years in the corporate bureaucracy of AT&T, Greenleaf likely knew that Servant-leading was not going to be an easy sell. Today, however, those who have studied his essays and other writings acknowledge that Greenleaf wrote with a prophetic voice about an emerging way of leading, and I suspect Greenleaf knew that any serious consideration of Servant-leading might kindle a greater awareness of a naturally human servant-consciousness.

Serving-first clearly contextualizes our motive, our purpose, and a way to lead, but for many that seems vague. Greenleaf did not provide an operational (empirical) definition for Servant-leading; in preference, he briefly referred to a feeling of wanting to serve-first, followed by a responsible, ethical, and humble choice to lead. Greenleaf (1996) defined leading as "going out ahead to show the way...to those situations in which the way is unclear or hazardous, or offers opportunities for creative achievement" (p. 12). His description of leading provides the essence for understanding what is expected of the Servant-leader. Leading is what Greenleaf was doing by proposing the need for Servant-leaders in our era.

Since Greenleaf's writings, many authors and researchers have attempted to clarify and operationalize Greenleaf's Servant-leader description. Interestingly, most new researchers (including myself) begin with attempts to redefine Servant-leading, as what Greenleaf offered seems vague and awkward, and imprecise. However, many of those who have been studying this philosophy for a while eventually return to and embrace Greenleaf's original statements. The reason, I suspect, is that Greenleaf was articulating something that is still clarifying in our minds and in our research. All of which supports the assertion that the philosophy is still emerging. Some qualitative clarifications and operational definitions are offered below as examples to show a span of perspectives and show some of the extent and the gaps in the mapping of the philosophy that research continues to fill in:

- Clarifying: Servant-leaders are those who "...*change the system, invent the new paradigm, and clear a space where something new can be. They accomplish this not just from 'doing' but more fundamentally, from 'being'...*" (Zohar, 1997, p. 146).
- Clarifying: *Servant-leadership is a state of mind, a philosophy of life, a way of being. It is at once an art and a calling* (Beazley, 2003, p. 10).
- Clarifying: *What separates Servant-leadership from other discussions of leadership is that fundamentally it concerns servants who lead, not leaders who serve* (Prosser, 2010, p. 42).
- Clarifying and operationalizing: The ten characteristics central to the development of Servant-leaders are *listening, empathy, healing, awareness, persuasion, conceptualization, foresight, stewardship, commitment to the growth of people, and building community* (Spears, 1998, pp. 5–8).
- Clarifying and operationalizing: *A Servant-leader is a person of character who puts people first. ...is a skilled communicator, a compassionate collaborator, has foresight, is a systems thinker, and leads with moral authority* (Sipe & Frick, 2009, p. 4).
- Operationalizing: *A Servant-leader:*

- *Values people by believing in people, serving other's needs before his or her own, and by receptive, non-judgmental listening.*
- *Develops people by providing opportunities for learning and growth, modeling appropriate behavior, and by building up others through encouragement and affirmation.*

- *Builds community by building strong personal relationships, working col-laboratively with others, and by valuing the differences of others.*
- *Displays authenticity by being open and accountable to others, a willing-ness to learn from others, and by maintaining integrity and trust.*
- *Provides leadership by envisioning the future, taking initiative, and by clarifying goals.*
- *Shares leadership by facilitating a shared vision, sharing power and releasing control, and by sharing status and promoting others.* (Laub, 1999, p. 83)

Laub was one of the first to develop an operational definition focused on what Servant-leaders do (or have done); although very helpful, these kinds of definitions do not directly measure *being* or the development of being from which the *natural feeling* of wanting to serve arises. In time since, other operational definitions of Servant-leadership continue to be developed. Certainly, we gain valuable insights and knowledge from these efforts to clarify and operationally measure Servant-leader effectiveness; however, there is more to understanding, developing, and practicing Servant-leadership.

Efforts to clarify and operationalize Servant-leadership reveal that our understanding of Servant-leading encompasses both *being* and *doing*. Becoming a Servant-leader and doing Servant-leadership is about devel-oping our *being* in a profoundly relational, creative, holistic, and inte-grated way so that the attitudinal dispositions, capacities, values, and skills for Servant-leadership manifest in our doing. The search for valid and reliable indicators of Servant-leadership is ongoing and I expect it will continue for some time, as it is still an emerging philosophy.

Transforming Leadership

One of the more academically confusing issues with Servant-leadership revolves around the question, what is the difference between Servant-leadership and transformational leadership? Many researchers have strug-gled to clarify and differentiate transformational leadership from Servant-leadership in their efforts to design empirical definitions and measuring instruments. From the perspective of Greenleaf's *Servant as*

Leader, most operational definitions tend to define Servant-leadership more narrowly than Greenleaf envisioned and tend to dilute and particularize the philosophy. The efforts to differentiate Servant-leading from transformational leading tend to set up an either/or preference; this is unfortunate as Servant-leadership is inherently transforming as it is a profoundly relational, creative, holistic, and integrative philosophy.

Greenleaf emphasized that Servant-leadership is about caring and hope and is focused on the growth and success of the individual, the organization, and society in general. "At its core, servant leadership is a long term, transformational approach to life and work-in essence, a way of being-that has potential for creating positive change throughout our society" (Greenleaf, 1998, p. 5). The philosophy assumes human, organizational, systems, and societal development entails transforming capacities. Servant-leaders may utilize developmental and transforming processes for specific objectives and general goals. Servant-leaders use processes and applications that may focus on the individual, team, group, organization, the community, or global society in general. An inclusive micro, meso, macro, mundo systems approach to development requires the assumption and understanding of the nature and processes of human and organizational transformation.

Servant-Leaders in Training

I have often wrestled with my own resistance in my struggle to introduce and conceptualize Servant-leadership. Through this struggle, I have increasingly become aware of the simplicity and paradoxically the complexity of Servant-leadership. Too often, I have become embarrassingly aware of how challenging it is to personally identify with what Greenleaf called that *natural feeling*, let alone consistently yearn to *serve-first*. I have often been humbled by the challenge to model Servant-leadership in work groups and even more so at the broader organizational level. The most perplexing challenges have been my efforts to model Servant-leading with my spouse, my children, and my grandchildren. I have learned over and over again that knowing and believing in some principles does not make one an expert practitioner. Reflecting on these experiences, I came to realize that I was only at the beginning of a servant-learning journey, and I felt much more comfortable acknowledging that I was actually a *Servant-leader in training*.

So now, I invite all who are interested in taking this learning journey to do the same. Becoming a *Servant-leader in training* is a true and worthy human quest. I have found that the simple acknowledgment that we are all in training to be Servant-leaders provides the freedom to not be perfect, to not get caught in absolutes, and to explore, experiment, struggle, make mistakes, reflect, and continue to enhance our awareness as we progress on this most naturally human and yet challenging, and transforming, way of being in the world.

Based on my understanding of human and leadership development, I am convinced that most of us, whether we are aware of it or not, are naturally in training to become Servant-leaders. Becoming a Servant-leader in training eventually involves the conscious development of a profoundly relational, creative, holistic, and integrative worldview. The integrative notion implies continuous internal searching for greater awareness, harmony, wisdom, and clarity. While integrative efforts seek infinite interior clarity and congruence, the yearning for holism nurtures our interior and exterior search for greater experience and knowledge of an ever expanding and evolving worldview.

Coming to view Servant-leadership as a natural organic philosophy is based on observations that from wherever we begin learning, understanding, and practicing Servant-leading, we find that it becomes more engaging and more conceptually and relationally challenging. Learning to become a Servant-leader is a developmental process—a process that enhances our awareness, our authenticity, our integrity, and in turn our relational capacity to respond to others. The conceptual struggle to understand and practice Servant-leadership is in itself evidence that Servant-leadership is more than a mere concept, a style, or a theory of leadership but rather an emerging worldview, a philosophy—a way of being in the world.

The struggle to understand Servant-leadership becomes immediately evident when we begin to review the ten characteristics Larry Spears drew from Greenleaf's writing (awareness, conceptualizing, empathizing, healing, listening, with a commitment to people, building community, and using foresight, persuasion, and stewardship). Today the number of characteristics continues to be in flux. Currently the number of research-based characteristics seems to be ranging from 6 to 17 depending on the authors and the focus of their research.

In my teaching experience, I have found that the tendency to immediately focus on the characteristics of Servant-leaders becomes prescriptive rather than developmental; nonetheless, the characteristics are important, as they are indicators of a richer understanding of the philosophy. Accordingly, before clarifying, describing, and learning how to apply and measure the characteristics, we should first attempt a greater depth of understanding of what might influence the development of a servant-consciousness, as presumably it reflects the fruit within which the dispositions, capacities, and characteristics might be found.

A servant-consciousness arises from serving-first, is inherently transforming, and is inspired by compassion, generosity, gratitude, and joy. A servant-consciousness reflects a leadership disposition that is profoundly relational, creative, holistic, and integrative. Attitudinal dispositions refer to overarching value structures that constitute the philosophy of Servant-leadership as reflected within human development. The primary capacities that influence Servant-leader development include moral authority, promoting community, listening-first, pathfinding-foresight, and systems thinking: these are the capacities to be stimulated, nurtured, and practiced as Servant-leaders in training. There may be other contributing capacities; however, these capacities seem most formative of a servant-consciousness—at this time. There are numerous interrelated values and skills associated with the dispositions and capacities; many are listed in Table 1.1. A quick search of Table 1.1 will reveal that the ten characteristics, and more, are embedded within the capacities, values, and skills (affirming that nothing is being lost).

Developing a servant-consciousness also involves learning and practicing a transforming dynamic I refer to as *aware healing* and *creative learning*. Aware healing and creative learning (more explicitly described in Chap. 6) are highly beneficial for holistic and integrative learning, and for paradigmatic growth shifts that arise from our experience of doing and being, and which flow from a profoundly relational warmhearted love of self and others. Aware healing implies surrendering our resistance, barriers, bias, and prejudice to learning and consciously opening to love.

I first became aware of the abundant creative nature of love when my second child was born. I was naively concerned that now that a new child had arrived I would have to share my love between two. Happily, this was not my experience; love is not finite and divisible. Love is indivisible, it radiates and is inherently inclusive, and it flows and evolves with each new emergence—and changes everything. The formation of a servant-consciousness changes our view of everything; it is undeniably an evolving journey, a journey all Servant-leaders in training are destined to begin.

Figure 1.2 is based on and adds perspective to Wilber's *four-quadrant model*. The spiral growth figure represents an individual's potential for growth from birth through four stages of development. The figure shows Stage I and II (1st Tier) fully developed with Stage III still developing and Stage IV emerging (2nd Tier), implying that growth is ongoing. Scharmer's (2009) four organizing structures are shown. The light and dark tubes running through and around in the bell represent the personal and the relational (Wilber's quadrants 1 and 2). The burgeoning spiral figure depicts that as we develop individual's growth is multidirectional as

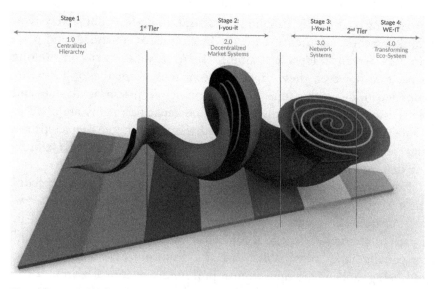

Fig. 1.2 Individual and collective development. Printed with permission of Gonzaga University

the complexity of our values and skills and conscious awareness increases. The (disproportionate) trapezoid-like bed in the figure represents the humanities collective heritage, the intersubjective cultural worldviews, and our environment and social systems (Wilber's quadrants 3 and 4). The wide base of the trapezoid depicts that the bulk of humanity has existed in the earlier stages of development, and fewer members of humanity have attained Stage IV.

The Leadership Crisis

Over the last 150 years and more, profits, philosophers, and other writers have suggested that humanity is involved in a huge developmental shift. Some recent researchers claim we are on the verge of a new renaissance (Goldin & Kutarna, 2017) evident in our current experience of a need for re-clarification of identity, meaning, and purpose expressed through changing values and skills and their manifestation within our social systems, organizations, and communities. Our systems and organizations have never been more complex nor perplexingly more fragmented and out of alignment with what they are attempting to do. Our systems and organizations are in great need of value clarification and system adjustments. We are in great need of a more expansive personal global systems framework and a guiding leadership framework with a priority on nurturing greater human flourishing.

Greenleaf began writing about a "crisis of leadership" in the early 1970s, claiming institutional administrators were choosing the wrong kind of leaders. Greenleaf (1977) posed that the leadership crisis had developed from an inappropriate focus on the importance of administrator perfection, too much attention on analytical problem solving, and too much self-protection and self-promotion. Servant-leading was proposed as a solution to the crisis. Nevertheless, there is little doubt that confidence in the leadership of Western institutions continues to decline.

Scharmer (2009) helps explain the complexity of our leadership problem, specifying that our educational training has not kept abreast, let alone ahead, of the increasing changes in organizational structures, systems design, and the demands and expectations of ways to successfully lead complex organizations today. Where formerly organizations were built on the assumptions of the centralized rational structure with hierarchal governance, today, we also have organizations designed on the assumptions of the decentralized market structures focused on service-oriented leadership. More recently, network structures have emerged that require trust, dialog, and facilitative leadership, and now organizing structures are evolving toward eco-structures that assume a truly open system with an even greater capacity for collaborative, adaptive, and creative leadership. Scharmer and Kaufer (2013) indicated that a major aspect of the leadership crisis is that we have all four of these kinds of governing structures functioning in our societies, and situationally sometimes all within the same organization. Each of these four structural systems has different fundamental assumptions, purposes, values, and need requirements for success and efficiency. In practice, the roles, skills, values, and perspectives of the leader and the leadership group, as well as the follower groups, can be dramatically different within each of the four governing structures. So, it is no wonder leadership theorists have had difficulty defining a general theory of leadership. We need a more comprehensive developmental theory of leadership.

Scharmer indicates that each prior structure is foundational for the next, in other words from the central hierarchy onward each successive structure becomes foundational and integral to the next; this means that the centralized hierarchal structure is not to be eliminated—nor frowned upon. More importantly, when a new more complex structure emerges (i.e., transitioning forms a central hierarchy to a market system, or a market system to a network system), the former structure needs to be redesigned and reframed and led so that it now fundamentally serves the flourishing of the more open and complex structure. Not doing this frustrates system efficiencies, and leadership and followership alike.

One of the primary roles for Servant-leaders in training is to integrate and harmonize the structures within the organizational systems, and that requires learning and understanding human development and systems complexity. To that end, Servant-leaders need to grow within themselves a global systems perspective and a capacity to work with a global systems framework. Today, such a framework requires a cosmic worldview, a more expansive worldview than the structures we are attempting to integrate.

The persistence of the ongoing leadership crisis is also a *leadership development* crisis (Bolt, 1996; Kegan & Lahey, 2009). New and more complex leadership values and skills are required for leading each successive organizational structure. It should not be surprising that leadership as a "school of study" has emerged only since the 1970s due to a growing need for leaders with relational and emotional maturity. It is not news that relational maturity is required to expedite the increasing need for collaboration in resolving organizations and systems issues. Nor is it news that emotional intelligence and other attributes that nurture and promote community require some advanced education and training.

Kegan and Lahey (2009) emphasized the need for leadership development, claiming that simply having the capacity to deal with the complexity in our organizations is an immense intellectual human development challenge. They claimed that currently our organizations need employees to be self-authoring (responsibly independent) and most employees are not. Most leaders today are expected to be self-transforming while only a few are. The expectation for our mental capacities falls way short of what our minds are actually capable of accomplishing. These claims point to a great leadership development challenge. The challenge is for individual leaders to develop a global systems capacity and a framework for understanding, facilitating, and transforming organizational change. This is a major challenge that needs to be intentionally attended to; equally important, leaders need to have the capacity and the care and willingness to call forth the development of others. Relationally, at the educative level, we need to focus on building interior cognitive, emotional, and moral capacities within ourselves and learn to collaboratively practice and model those values and skills in our collective systems.

How do we grow these capacities and become more holistic and integrated in ourselves, so that we can function within the complexity of the centralized, decentralized marketing, networked, and the emerging eco-structures? We need a more holistic and integrated awareness of our capacities of mind, heart, and body. If we are to avoid becoming overwhelmed as our organizations and societies strive to adapt to the burgeoning proliferation of information, we need to enhance our conscious capacity and use feelings and sensing to influence our reasoning. One of the major problems with increasing complexity is that it threatens to fragment our current worldview, and so we cling to what we know more tightly, worsening the crisis. The human development perspective on the leadership crises takes us to the heart of the issue.

Human development theorists acknowledge that a large portion of humanity (globally) is undergoing a fundamental values shift from the traditional hierarchical order toward demands for increased freedom, initiative, and human dignity. This values shift requires the personal integration of higher order complex values that nurture and support the independence and collaborative interdependence of self-initiating and self-responsible, self-transforming followers and leaders. Developing more Servant-leaders involves more than choosing and learning a different leadership style; it requires a profound shift in values such that a person's actual consciousness and worldview changes. The shift involves introspection, reflection, healing, learning, and a growth of consciousness such that one's purpose and sense of meaning is fundamentally transformed toward a more expansive and profoundly more relational perspective.

Aspects of this shift include viewing the world as increasingly organic (creative), diverse, and dynamically interconnected. When relationships become the priority around which to organize, a respect-filled *I–You* relational dynamic emerges, and we nurture what will become an *independence–interdependence* dynamic. The dynamic commences from the realization that all meaning and purpose arises from the dynamism of vital relationships, a willingness to personally seek greater clarity of purpose and responsibly embrace that sense of purpose. When relationships become the primary principle for organizing, then we will strive to wholeheartedly commit to serving relationships (interdependence) and focus on learning how to enhance relationships, and that leads to learning how to better incorporate relational values into system design. Relationships flourish when there is respect, honesty, trust, and authenticity, whereas self-aggrandizement, coercion, and manipulation create distrust, resistance, pain, and dysfunction. Servant-leadership does not harbor tyranny, cruelty, coercion, oppression, lying, cheating, or swindling.

Leadership development requires not only relational and system knowledge and skills but also the integration of spiritual intelligences. Spears (1998) suggested the notion of serving is connected to the "deepest yearnings of the human spirit" (p. xii), making the foundational inspiration a choice to serve—to serve-first. Leaders today are called to draw on the spirit; to be reflective; derive meaning based on experience, knowledge, and inspired wisdom; and be creative. Leaders need to foster within themselves, and within others, a holistic perspective and a willingness to responsibly participate and not only act independently but also increasingly interdependently. Developmentally leaders today are called to learn skills and values that help predispose us to conceptualize and structure processes and systems that are more holistic and flexibly able to meet the challenges of a dynamic environment.

Servant-leadership was originally proposed, and continues to emerge, as the antidote to the crisis of leadership. What is most interesting is that the choice to serve-first adds a profoundly different perspective for leading. Servant-leading provides an inclusive relational perspective that changes the focus and the purpose of the centralized hierarchy, the decentralized market structure, and paves the way for the network structure, and eco-structures. The wisdom within this inclusive perspective has a transcending potential to revitalize organizations and society.

The Motive for Servant-Leadership

Coming to understand the motive to serve-first is part of the struggle for Servant-leaders in training. If choosing to serve-first is a legitimate predisposition for leading, what might be the motive behind Greenleaf's so-called natural feeling that inclines us to want to serve-first? And what is the pay off? Why serve? If there were no personal benefit, then it is likely not a natural feeling, and the idea of Servant-leadership would have naturally disappeared years ago.

Certainly, as mothers and fathers, serving the needs of our young and grown children, as well as our parents and grandparents, seems instinctual and natural. Additionally, we may yearn to serve our team, our unit, our group, our organization, our community to enrich our sense of belonging, self-worth, and purpose. Many yearn to serve a cause, a philosophy, a God. Incontestably, many choose to work and serve for different reasons, including for survival, duty, or obligation; for approval, or money, power, and influence; or sometimes because it is merely something to do.

Whatever the reason for serving, there is one thing I am quite certain about; being consciously aware of the *natural feeling* of wanting to serve-first is rarely acknowledged as felt, let alone well-articulated. What was Greenleaf referring to and how might we bring this *natural feeling* into greater awareness?

A way to begin is to reflect on our current experience and awareness of serving and being served. For instance, we might pay attention to and explore the natural feelings around the consequences of serving. To do this, reflectively call to mind the positive internal feelings that arise after you have performed an authentic act of service—an event where you freely served because it was the right thing to do. Is there an internal affirmation that arises from helping out a friend, or even a stranger, in need? Tempered with humility, these serving acts emerge from feelings of compassion, generosity, caring, and love, and to some extent, they nurture gratitude and joy.

Love for others, and self, is inherent within the motive for desiring to *serve-first*. As human beings we are created for relationships; relationships with others, with animals, nature, and all of creation. The paradox is that being in relationship is often awkward and painful, but it is through these relationships we become able to learn what is most meaningful and most human, even though we often fall far short of the mark. As we become more fully aware of our capacity for love, we are tested with the choices of whether or not to be honest, responsible, moral, generous, forgiving, and humble. Developing the capacity to hold loosely our judgments, our distrust, our doubt, and our fears and become present and available to another is an act of love, even though it may stir feelings of vulnerability. Being in relationship helps develop our emotional and spiritual maturity.

Humility is involved in serving-first. A leader who has the capacity to lead from both natural gifts (strengths) and humility (admitting mistakes, honesty, forgiving, and healing) has a much wider spectrum of options for effectiveness, and one's perceived authenticity may be significantly enhanced. Through love, as in being warmhearted versus cold-hearted, a leader has a greater capacity for authentic, respectful relating with others, and is better able to address and establish trust, and issues that promote worth, fulfillment, and purpose.

A second way to reflect on the *why serve* question is to recall the feelings of gratitude we have toward those who served us when we were in need, helpless, or powerless. Can you recall someone who offered a comforting word, a helping hand, or a great service, when you were compromised, lost, or vulnerable? And can you recall the sincere appreciation (gratitude, love) you felt for the unexpected acts of service toward you? These experiences nurture our capacity to honor others humbly, and to graciously receive.

A third awareness contributing to the natural feeling to want to serve-first is also related to the abundant nature of love. The more love there is, the more it radiates and flows, it is inherently indivisible, it is expansionary and inclusive. Similarly, there is also an abundant nature to (healthy) serving in that it inherently stimulates an inclination to *pass it on*. Passing it on may simply mean continuing being of service to others, or expressing more honoring awareness and sincerity in humbly receiving, or enhanced joy from influencing and witnessing others passing it on. Our desire to mentor and be mentored is an aspect of this kind of serving.

Can you recall times that stimulated wanting to *pass it on*? For example, can you recall a time when someone you respected treated *you* with *profound respect*, or perhaps a time when you received some form of a *blessing* from someone you highly esteemed. When you have passed on *respect* or a *blessing*, how did you feel? How does it feel when you have done a good job at *passing it on*? For some of us, these may be feelings we do not even have a specific name for. Often we tend to wave them off, or downplay them. For example, in response to someone's gratitude, we say "forget it, it was nothing"—but it was not no-thing. The affirming feelings associated with love, compassion, generosity, gratitude, and joy and wanting to *pass it on* connect us with others and influence our seeking opportunities to serve again. Awareness and a humble acknowledgment of these feelings help to develop our sense of authenticity and integrity. There seems to be something internally right about influencing people or situations in a positive way and doing good deeds—whether it is doing something for the benefit of a child, an organization, or an ecosystem.

Our appreciation of the compassion and generosity of others nurtures a desire to reciprocate, to contribute, and to serve the greater good. Our sense of rightness and duty creates an urge to take responsibility for at least our part of the world, moving us into action and respectful relationship with people, engendering, and ethic of love. Serving others enables us to overcome greed, fear, and egocentricity. Love engenders a servant-consciousness, which culminates in universal love.

Our awareness and experience of the natural feelings on both sides of the giving and receiving gratitude spectrum are important and need to be held in our awareness as Servant-leaders in training. The feelings of compassion, generosity, gratitude, and joy that arise from serving, being served, and passing it on affirm and enhance a balanced and humble sense of worth-fullness, a sense of affirming goodness, fulfillment, and meaning. Such awareness enhances our emotional capacity and helps us to understand the natural feeling for wanting to serve-first. These examples of serving seem to resonate with some sense of internal rightness; and they are quite conducive to transparency—at least from others, if not from ourselves. All this leads me to believe these feelings are signs of a more fundamental motive beneath the desire to serve-first.

The yearning to serve-first arises as an inspiration (Greenleaf, 1977), the inspiration ignites the motive, the motive attracts thought patterns (Zohar & Marshall, 2004), and the thought patterns echo our innate desire for greater wholeness. Wholeness, for Greenleaf, appears to be synonymous with healing. He made this point in one very brief but illuminating paragraph. "This is an interesting word, *healing*, with its meaning, 'to make whole.' ...one really never makes it. It is always something sought. ...the Servant-leader might acknowledge that his own healing is his motivation" (1977, p. 36). With these few words, Greenleaf communicated his understanding of the fundamental yearning and purpose for serving, and leading is to make ourselves whole—or at least to make ourselves more whole, and becoming more whole involves healing.

Greenleaf insightfully proposed that greater wholeness is the motive for Servant-leaders. He did not elaborate further; however, the implication is that if one is to achieve greater wholeness, then the obvious way is to become aware of and respond to an inspirational yearning *to serve-first*. Burns (2003) wrote:

Humans are motivated by wants and needs that are not only material but also a rich and complex mix of physical, psychological, social, sexual, wants and needs that are both inward, for self-fulfillment, self-actualization, and that also look outward for their satisfaction, through the achievement of some change in the world. (p. 15)

The motive for the Servant-leader appears to be first an outward movement for an inward sense of fulfillment and actualization. By choosing to serve, Servant-leaders in training are consciously responding to a yearning for greater wholeness. The notion that serving develops greater wholeness implies an outward movement that surpasses the desire for individual independence and extends toward greater interdependence in relationships, such that an intentional and responsible act toward another directly or indirectly serves the good of both *you* and *I*. A deliberate movement toward greater interdependence implies a yearning to deepen and enrich our relationships—and that likely involves some healing. Healing arises with compassion for ourselves and others, felt compassion evokes healing. Healing and wholeness are major themes for Servant-leaders in training (see aware healing and creative learning in Chap. 6).

Greater wholeness is a mutual endeavor. "There is something subtle communicated to one who is being served and led if, implicit in the compact between Servant-leader and led, is the understanding that the search for wholeness is something they share" (Greenleaf, 1977, p. 36). With these words, Greenleaf subtly melds the relational motive for Servant-leading with a mutually empathetic motive for those served. The intention of the choice to serve-first is deeply rooted in the desire for greater individual and relational wholeness, such that the intentions and acts of service may empathetically call forth (connect with a similar synchronistic) yearning for greater healing and wholeness in others: this is an indicator of the influential power of Servant-leadership.

Relational theories have been around for some time; however, as we become more aware of the depth of the call to Servant-leadership, we become aware that this relational philosophy is contextually, and archetypically, different than other relational theory—and the difference is that serving-first is profoundly relational. Servant-leadership is profoundly relational because it is first other oriented. Serving-first contextualizes our motive, the way, and the purpose and meaning of our leadership, and all that we do. With this awareness Servant-leaders strive to realize a profoundly relational leadership approach.

The interdependent nature of wanting to serve-first appears to be more socio-centric than ego-centric. Human development research indicates that developmentally humans have the natural capacity to grow from ego-centrism toward progressively more expansive and inclusive levels of socio-centrism (Wilber, 2006). Psychologically this involves growth from a very *ego-centric* it is all about me and mine, toward a more expansive and ethical us and them *ethno-centric* perspective, toward a *global-centric* all of us perspective, and eventually expanding to a *cosmic-centrism* that assumes we are all connected with everything. Each transformative shift involves profound developmental changes in the complexity of our values and skills, an expansion of our relational inclusivity, and an expansion of how we view our self, others, and the world.

Greenleaf's quest for greater mutual wholeness seems to arise from at least a global-centric perspective; the evidence is in his statement that choosing to serve-first was a natural feeling. It is unlikely that an ego-centric person striving for greater independence will have much awareness of the natural feeling to serve-first. Regarding ethno-centrism, Greenleaf set no limitation or qualification on who or what is to be served. Serving-first facilitates our development toward a global perspective. Developing global-centricity is about developing a serving disposition; however, it does not come without a struggle to integrate, evolve, and align our values and skills. In this sense, Greenleaf's description of a *natural* feeling may need to be practiced and modeled until it is felt as a natural yearning. To become a disposition serving-first needs to be concretized through repeated practice until it becomes a foundational to an integrated servant-consciousness. Thus, if serving-first seems unnatural, do it anyway, it will eventually become a primary way to engage the world.

Resistance Is the Gateway

The resistance to Servant-leadership that Greenleaf experienced when he first introduced this ancient yet still quite radical idea of serving-first continues. Every time I introduce Servant-leadership to graduate students, they begin with an internal struggle to overcome resistance and confusion about what they perceive leadership and Servant-leadership to mean and involve. Generally, attending to our resistance and becoming aware of our prejudices and barriers is a natural starting point for paradigmatic shifts, and as such intentionally attending to our resistance is a good place to begin to understand Servant-leadership. Struggling through our resistance bears much fruit and it affirms our capacity to develop a transforming consciousness.

Resistance is natural and serves a purpose; resistance creates awareness. The mystic, Willigis Jager (1995), indicates that our ego is so constructed that it has to resist, and without this tendency, there would be no human evolution (p. 203). Experience teaches that the prejudgments and emotional barriers that arise in our resistance to Servant-leadership often are the very barriers that need to be examined most closely, as they are the thresholds that lead to the insights that change our perspective and evolve our understanding and practice. Without the resistance we would not find our way. Loosening our hold on old leadership frameworks practicing being in the uneasiness of not-knowing allows for some disintegration (letting go) before new insights occur. We need to hold ourselves to this struggle until the creative insights and understandings begin to clarify, and a new worldview begins to emerge. Otherwise, without a full understanding of the assumptions and implications of Servant-leadership, we would not really know what is being rejected.

Greenleaf's suggestion that wanting to serve-first is a natural feeling often engenders resistance. Many of us associate the term serving with servitude. Resistance automatically arises as our understanding or experience of a *servant* quakes the depths of our very identity, and freedom, and raises cultural biases as well as embedded yearnings for independence, success, and power. Who wants to be a servant—to be servile? *Servitude is not on my list of career goal aspirations!* Nevertheless, if we push through those threats to our identity and independence, we come to realize Servant-leadership is about clarifying our authenticity and integrity and is a more expansive independent and interdependent relational perspective that is mutually self-empowering and other empowering.

Early attempts to understand and explain Servant-leadership to others can be awkward, because many of us attempt to re-conceptualize it using the familiar values and assumptions of the traditional leader; or we attempt to explain Servant-leadership in terms of values and skills we have not yet integrated into our own way of being. The result is the concepts of Servant-leadership may sound vague, and prejudgments arise— such as *it is soft touchy-feely, unrealistic, idealistic nonsense*. Because of this descriptive awkwardness and lack of clarity, many are tempted to reject Servant-leadership because it does not fit well with their standard operating vocabulary, or behavioral norms and experience within organizational culture.

Not everyone resists Servant-leadership. On first hearing of the term, some people immediately resonate with it and find it to be quite exciting—even compelling. After a closer examination, however, predictable reactions occur. Servant-leaders in training soon find many of their preconceptions were naïve, undeveloped, or simply wrong—there is much more to Servant-leadership than they first perceived. Others agree that Servant-leadership sounds nice and it may work in some organizations, in some situations—in churches and non-profits perhaps, but certainly not, for example, in the military, or *the shark pond where I work*!

A subtler resistance that arises and impedes adoption of the notion of serving-first is the misassumption that to become a Servant-leader, one must become completely selfless. In religious circles, selflessness is often brandished as an ideal; yet, we often distort what is meant by selflessness fearing a loss of identity and meaning. "Acting upon the impulse to serve others does not mean one is a 'service provider' a martyr or a slave, but one who consciously nurtures the mature growth of self, other people, institutions, and communities" (Sipe & Frick, 2009, p. 38). Choosing to serve involves a selflessness that resides between the extreme of self-abandonment and a lack of self-centeredness.

A total loss of boundaries occurs with self-abandonment, which leads to the possibility of being taken over by the needs and desires of others, while the one taking over feels he or she is actually being of service. After a time, one who has served others in this manner becomes completely confused and feels an inner emptiness. On the other hand, placing oneself at the center of whatever one does, making sure that personal benefit of one sort or another results, leaves the person or institution being 'served' in this manner empty. (Sardello, 2012, p. 13)

Much of what we do for others tends to be a version of self-serving, approval seeking, egotism that is often mistaken for selflessness. Intuitively and experientially, we know that ego gratification bears unfulfilling fruit in our search for greater meaning and purpose. Yet, selflessness does not mean becoming egoless. A balanced healthy sense of selflessness reflects an aware healing and creative learning capacity with the empathy to be other oriented. To keep the balance, Sardello (2012) suggests "the ego needs to be given a sacred task" (p. 13). The sacred task we are to give the ego is to serve, to serve-first. Developing a servant-consciousness involves transforming our ego orientation from self-serving to serving-first.

Creatively Exploring the I–You Concept

As Servant-leaders in training, understanding the potential for a continuously expanding capacity for relationship is a significant insight. How might we creatively grow our capacity for greater socio-centricity? A conceptual perspective might sound like this: the Servant-leader consciously chooses to serve, motivated by an empathetic and gratuitous feeling toward others and a yearning for greater wholeness. Imaginatively, let us attempt to bring these feelings and thoughts to the conscious level: *I humbly realize that greater relational interdependence is essential to my greater wholeness, your greater wholeness, and our greater wholeness.* The relational dynamic becomes enriched synergistically when it is knowingly and mutually acknowledged. This realization adds even more impact, awareness, and resolve to the choice to serve as it evokes choice, engagement, and a moral responsibility to respectfully serve for the greater good of both, and to some extent each serves the other. The moral responsibility of the relationship is mutual and moves us toward greater authenticity and humility.

With further inspiration from Martin Buber's *I-Thou* relational dynamic, let us take this imaginative perspective a little further. *If I am to continue to experience greater wholeness as a Servant-leader in training, my service needs to be focused on my serving You* (the 2nd person You refers to any person, group, organization, community, society, or ecosystem). Capitalizing the y in You signifies a profound qualitative shift in awareness of the value of the relationship. This enriched notion reflects more equality and responsible appreciation, such that *I perceive Your dignity is worthy of my deepest and humblest respect, and I view Our relationship as necessary for My, Your and Our greater wholeness.* Developmentally my *I* does not diminish, or disappear. I do not become completely selfless, or become insignificant; rather I realize a developmental clarification—an expanded clarified perspective where self-centeredness diminishes through (transforming) awareness and a more magnanimous socio-centric *I* emerges. An *I* that is more authentic, transparent, and humble; an *I* that is more available to relationship. Simultaneously my appreciation and value for *You* magnifies significantly, as I gain a richer perception and appreciation for *You. I* become aware that *You* are central to my further growth, your further growth, and our greater flourishing. I become more available to relationship, and because of our mutual awareness (potentially), so do *You*, and together an even more dynamic relational potentiality occurs. What this means is that *I* plus *You* in effect produce a clarified and enhanced collective *We* relationship. Where neither *I* nor *You* are diminished because of the relationship. Relationally, serving each other synergistically creates a greater whole.

One more time, the *natural* feeling is intrinsically intended toward greater relationship, such that there must be an acknowledged interdependent aspect to this motive if it is to be most fruitful. The choice to serve is about enhancing our wholeness individually and collectively. Servant-leadership is about *You* and *I* becoming more fully human individually and collectively; in the fullest sense this means that the fruit of serving is the enhancement of the collective *We/It*. (*We/It* here represents Wilber's (2006) two lower quadrants, cultural knowledge and organizing systems).

Choosing to serve-first helps bring our desire for wholeness to greater fruition. Similar to the notion that happiness is a by-product of right living, greater personal and relational wholeness comes as a by-product of serving. By authentically striving to serve others, our well-being is enhanced, and we often feel more fulfilled than drained, as we get back more than we give. Thus, the statement serving is more meaningful and more self-fulfilling than self-serving is (Keith, 2008). Greater wholeness includes awareness and greater integrations of the implications of *I, You,* and *We/It* (1st person, 2nd person, 3rd person). Whether this transformation occurs slowly over time, or in an instant, a profound transformation occurs when we shift from centering on *I* to centering on *I–You* and *We/It*; *I* am no longer self-absorbed.

The motive originates in the self and calls forth a somewhat similar motive in others. Thus, a Servant-leader intuitively or openly acknowledges, values, and nurtures relationships as opposed to manipulating, using, abusing, coercing, or destroying them. Nurturing relationships creates stability and trust. Serving and valuing this relational dynamic is integral to a Servant-leader's worldview. Servant-leadership is first other oriented, and as a result, the serving disposition has a different trajectory, the disposition carries a different payload of value priorities. Serving-first deploys differently than choosing to lead for power or recognition, and therefore the outcomes will not only bear fruit differently, but will bear different fruit and, over time (as the research evidence affirms) will bear more abundant fruit than traditional leadership.

With all that stated, Servant-leadership may well be the most challenging, the most comprehensive, and the most complex form of leadership, and it may be *true leadership*—a form of leadership that requires deliberate, mindful practice and development. As a philosophy, Servant-leadership assumes a profoundly relational other-oriented stance and a moral framework that seeks a holistic and integrative worldview that becomes a way of approaching and doing all personal, relational, and organizational functions.

References

Beazley, H. (2003). Forward. In H. Beazley, J. Beggs, & L. C. Spears (Eds.), *The servant-leader within: A transformative path* (pp. 1–11). New York: Paulist Press.

Beck, D. E., & Cowan, C. C. (1996/2006a). *Spiral dynamics: Mastering values, leadership, and change*. Malden, MA: Blackwell.

Bolt, J. F. (1996). Developing three-dimensional leaders. In F. Hesselbein, M. Goldsmith, & R. Bechard (Eds.), *The leader of the future* (pp. 161–173). San Francisco: Jossey-Bass.

Burns, J. M. (2003). *Transforming leadership: A new pursuit of happiness.* New York: Atlantic Monthly Press.

Goldin, I., & Kutarna, C. (2017). *Age of discovery: Navigating the risks and rewards of our new renaissance.* Bloomsbury: St. Martin's Press.

Greenleaf, R. K. (1977). *Servant leadership: A journey into the nature of legitimate power and greatness.* New York: Paulist Press.

Greenleaf, R. K. (1996). Religious leaders as seekers and servants. In A. T. Fraker & L. C. Spears (Eds.), *Seeker and servant: Reflections on religious leadership* (pp. 9–48). San Francisco: Jossey-Bass.

Greenleaf, R. K. (1998). *The power of Servant Leadership.* San Francisco: Berrett-Koehler.

Hall, B. P. (1994). *Values shift: A guide to personal & organizational transformation.* Rockport, MA: Twin Lights.

Jager, W. (1995). *Search for the meaning of life: Essays and reflections on the mystical experience.* Liguori, MO: Liguori/Triumph.

Kegan, R., & Lahey, L. L. (2009). *Immunity to change.* Boston, MA: Harvard Business Press.

Keith, K. (2008). *The case for servant leadership.* Westfield, IN: The Greenleaf Center for Servant Leadership.

Laub, J. A. (1999). *Assessing the servant-organization: Development of the servant organizational leadership assessment (SOLA) instrument.* Doctoral dissertation, Florida Atlantic University.

Prosser, S. (2010). *Servant leadership: More philosophy, less theory.* Westfield, IN: Greenleaf Center.

Sardello, R. (2012). *The power of the soul: Living the twelve virtues.* Benson, NC: Goldenstone Press.

Scharmer, O. (2009). *Theory U: Leading from the future as it emerges.* San Francisco: Berrett-Koehler.

Scharmer, O., & Kaufer, K. (2013). *Leading from the emerging future: From ego-system to eco-system economies*. San Francisco: Barrett-Koehler.

Sipe, J. W., & Frick, D. M. (2009). *Seven pillars of servant leadership: Practicing the wisdom of leading by serving*. New York: Paulist Press.

Spears, L. C. (1995). Servant leadership and the Greenleaf legacy. In L. C. Spears (Ed.), *Reflections on leadership: How Robert K. Greenleaf's theory of servant-leadership influenced today's top management thinkers* (pp. 1–14). New York: John Wiley & Sons.

Spears, L. C. (1998). Tracing the growing impact of servant-leadership. In L. C. Spears (Ed.), *Insights on leadership: Service, stewardship, spirit, and servant-leadership* (pp. 1–11). New York: John Wiley & Sons.

Thompson, M. C. (2000). *The congruent life: Following the inward path to fulfilling work and inspired leadership*. San Francisco: Jossey-Bass.

Wilber, K. (2001). *A theory of everything: An integral vision for business, politics, science, and spirituality*. Boston, MA: Shambala.

Wilber, K. (2006). *Integral spirituality: A startling new role for religion in the modern world*. Boston, MA: Integral Books.

Zohar, D. (1997). *Rewiring the corporate brain: Using the new science to rethink how we structure and lead organizations*. San Francisco: Berrett-Koehler Publishing.

Zohar, D., & Marshall, I. (2004). *Spiritual capital: Wealth we can live by*. San Francisco: Barrett-Koehler.

2

Human Development

A Development Framework

Human development theorists show that the human experience from birth to death can be viewed as a developmental journey. "…man develops. Whatever he is at present, he was not always so, and generally speaking he need not remain so" (Lonergan in Morelli & Morelli, 2002, p. 254). Just as each human has the potential to grow into new stages of development, they also have the opportunity to develop their leadership. Developmentally, the Servant-leader emerges as a leader typology in the human growth journey.

To provide a holistic perspective, several human development models are drawn from to help generalize and locate the philosophy of Servant-leadership in a developmental framework. The models structure the human development journey and show how and where leadership typologies emerge on the journey. The models assume each human born into this world may potentially experience a number of distinct, sequential, and invariable stages of growth (Wilber, 2006). An explicit assumption is that all fundamental change begins at the spiritual level first; thus, each stage of development begins with spiritual inspiration and involves

© The Author(s) 2018
J. H. Horsman, *Servant-Leaders in Training*,
Palgrave Studies in Workplace Spirituality and Fulfillment,
https://doi.org/10.1007/978-3-319-92961-3_2

holistic development at progressively broader, more expansive, and deeper levels. The exact number of stages (or phases) varies somewhat among the models. For our purposes, we focus on four stages. Progress through the potential stages of development involves three profound shifts. Each unique shift initiates and involves a paradigmatic change in our world-view. A successful shift involves learning, practicing, and integrating a number of progressively more complex values and skills; these values and skills are associated with distinct leadership typologies. What makes these stages developmental is that each prior stage is a necessary foundation for growth to the next.

Table 2.1 is an (approximate) comparative categorization of ten human development theories (several more could have been included). Table 2.1 shows stages, tiers, developmental transitions, and spiritual transitions. The relative similarities of developmental categorizations for individual development can be observed between models. The numerous categorizations of development generally reflect similar value connotations in each stage of development. The table shows four distinct stages of developmental running from left to right. Below the stages Beck and Cowan's 1st and 2nd Tiers (a 3rd Tier beyond Stage IV is not represented here) show an approximate association with the four stages. Below the stages Rolheiser's three spiritual transitions are represented, followed by Kegan and Lahey's socialized mind, self-authoring mind, and transforming mind, and then dependence, independence, and independence–interdependence again in approximate association with the stages. The next rows show six development models beginning with Fowler's categories of faith development. Well-known models produced by Kohlberg, Loevinger et al., Torbert and Fisher/Rooke, and Maslow, Zohar, and Marshal are then presented to show relative similarities in the models. Wilber's developmental categories are the last shown (the >> in the row signifies ongoing human development).

Table 2.2 shows that each stage consists of an A and B focus. The A stage represents an internal focus on learning personal values and skills, and the B stages represents a focus on learning to apply those values in relationships (i.e., collective development tends to lag personal development). The following row juxtaposes four levels of socio-centrism, followed by Scharmer's four governing structures. The next two rows display

Table 2.1 Relating human development

Human Development	Stage I		Stage II		Stage III		Stage IV	
	1st Tier				2nd Tier			
Beck & Cowan								>>
Kegan & Lahey Socialized Mind	Socialized Mind		Self-authoring Mind				Transforming Mind	
	Dependence				Independence		*Independence—Interdependence	
Rolheiser Spiritual transitions			<- Getting our life together		<- Giving our life away		<- Giving our death away	
Fowler Primal Faith	Magic	Mythic	Conventional Faith	Individuated Reflective	Conjunctive Faith		Universalizing-commonwealth	
	Magic	Literal						
Kohlberg	Fear	Self-interest	Conventional Conformity		Post-Conventional			
Pre-Conventional			Social Order		Others Rights		Universal Principal	
Torbert & Fisher/Rooke	Impulsive - Opportunist		Diplomat	Technician - Expert	Achiever	Individualist	Strategist	Alchemist
								Visionary
Loevinger	Symbolic	Impulsive	Self-Protective	Conformist	Conscientious	Individualist	Autonomous	Integrated / Ego Aware
Maslow's Needs Hierarchy	Survival, Food, Warmth, Shelter		Achievement: Self-Worth, Competence & Success Ego		Self-Actualizing: Meaning Transcendence, Creativity		Peak Experiences	
Zohar/Marshall	Exploration	Gregarious	Power Within	Mastery	Generativity	Higher service	World Soul	Enlightened
Beck/Cowan Basic	Magical Mystical	Impulsive Power	Purposeful Saintly	Strategic Materialist	Sensitive Humanistic		Integrative Ecological	Holistic Global
Wilber	Instinctual	Magic	Ego	Mythic	Achiever	Pluralistic	Holistic	Integral >>

*Author's insertion; >> implies ongoing development

Table 2.2 Stages of development

Human Development	Stage I		Stage II		Stage III		Stage IV	
	IA	**IB**	**IIA**	**IIB**	**IIIA**	**IIIB**	**IVA**	**IVB**
Hall	Safety Self-preservation	Security Family	Self-worth Belonging	Confidence Competence	Self-actualization	Vocation New Systems	*Collective-actualization	Global Wisdom
	Ego-centric		Ethno-centric		Global-centric		Cosmic-centric	
Scharmer Structures	1.0 Centralized Control		Competitive 2.0 Market System		Collaborative 3.0 Network System		All Source Open 4.0 Eco-System	
Hall: Followers	Oppressed	Preserver	Loyal Subordinate	Interpersonal & Searching	Creative Independent		Creative Serve-first	*Generative-servants
Hall: Leader	Autocrat	Benevolent Autocrat	Manager	Enabler	Collaborator		Servant	*Generative-servant

1st Tier — **Leader Typologies** — **2nd Tier**

------ *Servant-leaders in training* ------>>

Tribal-leader - Autocrat - Bureaucrat/Admin - Manager - Communitarian - Servant-leader - Generative-servant

Adapted from Hall (1994) and Scharmer and Kaufer (2013)
*Author's insertion, different from Hall's typology

Hall's follower and leader categorizations that emerge within and between the developmental stages. The final row shows a variation of leader typologies drawn from a mix of the models with my rendition of Servant-leader and Generative-servant. The bottom row shows *Servant-leaders in training* as developmentally we are all potentially preparing to become Servant-leaders. Also, as Servant-leaders in training, we can serve-first at any stage of development and finally that we potentially have access to all four stages at any point in time. Servant-leading emerges as a disposition in Stage III and continues to develop through Stage IV. A servant-consciousness may emerge in Stage IIIB and develop through Stage IV.

Although there are volumes of information behind Tables 2.1 and 2.2, the two tables can be used as a background overview of the human development assumptions that support the Servant-leaders in training concepts. Even though the terminology may vary between models, the Servant-leader is a distinct typology that consistently emerges in Stage III development. What the models show is that Servant-leader values and skills naturally come into greater fruition during Stage III and continue into Stage IV. Importantly, developmental assumptions suggest that if the values and skills pertinent to Stages I and II are not developed, they will not come to fruition in Stage III.

The human development models reveal that Servant-leading is a natural evolution of leadership. Normally we progress, from tribal elders to autocrat to benevolent autocrats or paternal/maternal leaders, and as organizations become more bureaucratic and complex administrative management and supportive participative leaders emerge, today participative collaborative Servant-leaders and Generative-servants are being called for. Wilber (2006) claimed the bulk of organizations in Western society are in the Achiever stage (see Table 2.1) with some organizations testing the Pluralistic and the Holistic stages of development. If that is so, the tables show that a Servant-leader typology will continue to emerge as it is to some extent still on the frontier of organizational development. Note all types of 2nd Tier leadership beyond Stage IIIA will be variations of the Servant-leader.

Although Servant-leaders normally grow through the sequential leadership typologies, that does not exclude anyone from serving-first at any stage of development. Certainly, some people may seem to have exhibited a Servant-leader approach for much of their lives; however, even brief histories of Gandhi, Mother Teresa, Nelson Mandela, or Pope Francis reveal evidence of developmental growth. Importantly, the evolving nature of human development and leadership, although natural, is not automatically determined by experience or aging. To progress developmentally values and skills need to be yearned for, strived for, successfully learned, practiced, and integrated.

Similarly to individual development, an evolution of collective organizing structures and systems (usually with some collective lag) is quite evident in our organizational and system design. The organizing structures reveal priorities and values that roughly correspond to each stage of development (see Table 2.2, Scharmer). For example, organizations disseminate power and decision authority from the centralized hierarchy to the decentralized market system, to the network systems, to the emerging ecosystems (Scharmer & Kaufer, 2013). Also, note that within the follower and leader categories (Table 2.2) after Stage IIIA, leaders become more open to a *first among equals* (Greenleaf) approach to organizing as the follower–leader role is experienced as interchanging. The general pattern reveals that as our capacity for increasing complexity enhances, our systems and structures become more open, more inclusive, and diversity is valued while power is dispersed and modifies toward influence. As the systems become more diverse, they potentially become more inclusive, more adaptive, and more integrative, and dare I say more human.

The formation of a Servant-leader disposition is a journey all Servant-leaders in training are destined to at least begin, and coming to understand Servant-leadership is an evolving learning process. The more we struggle to put into practice the assumptions, concepts, perspectives, and responsibilities of Servant-leadership, the clearer they become. Prosser (2010) suggested that this evolution was evident in Greenleaf's own writings, which showed signs of evolving from an experiential theory toward an emerging philosophy. A similar evolution is ongoing with many others who are engaged in learning to practice and teach Servant-leadership. Awareness of the extent of the journey, and gaining a sense of where we are developmentally, is certainly helpful, and part of the purpose of using the models. Hence, with a little research on human development, and some assessment (not included here), we can locate ourselves on the leadership spectrum, as well as our leaders, and our organizing structures.

Regardless of our current stage of development, new worldviews seldom emerge without some struggle, adaptation, and much learning. Wilber (2006) describes the formation of a new worldview as the concretizing of our states of awareness into a new foundational stage of development. So, becoming a Servant-leader in training has all the ensuing challenges associated with integrating a more comprehensive way of being, acting, and viewing the world, and that entails natural transformative growth processes. The struggle to learn and conceptualize Servant-leadership may be like experiencing a paradigmatic shift, such as shifting from a mechanistic perspective to a quantum perspective, where we have to hold in abeyance what we think we know, add some insights, learn new facts and practices, and reorganize it all into a more expansive, integrated, and complex perspective.

Stages of Human Development

The crisis of leadership has been referred to as a leadership development crisis. Kegan and Lahey (2009) suggested part of the problem is that leadership studies have "over attended to leadership and under-attended to development" (p. 5). Traditionally, management literature begins the discussion of leadership with explanations of Theory X and Theory Y; however, a lot more is involved than just an either/or orientation. Studying leadership through a human development framework provides more context for understanding the evolving nature of leadership. The models also help us identify the dispositions, capacities, values, and skills required for personal and organizational progress.

The human development models were developed from a variety of perspectives, that is, moral, philosophical, psychological, sociological, spiritual, and value perspectives. Needless to say, I have edited much of the theory with the aim of providing (as briefly as possible) a skeletal framework to understand the background of the complexity and the maturity required of Servant-leaders. Importantly, there is much more to the developmental theories than what is presented here, a study of human development ought to be foundational to any leadership development program. What is presented here is at best a minimum framework for understanding the importance of the models as they relate to leadership development.

Hall (1994) categorized human development into four major worldviews or stages (phrases) of development. A primary purpose for the emphasis on the models is to show that Servant-leadership is a legitimate leadership typology for Stage III–IV leadership. It is also an appropriate leadership typology for leading those who are at Stages I, II, III, and IV. In other words, as *Servant-leaders in training*, there is an all-inclusive leadership purpose and benefit for learning leadership development.

A four-stage framework of worldviews is not new, in fact, it is ancient. Some Native American mythologies, for example, describe human development in terms of four ages: childhood, young adult, adulthood, and the age of wisdom. See Fig. 2.1; the circular pictorial prefigures Fig. 1.2 (Chap. 1) and is an early view into the bell of the spiral.

Viewing Fig. 2.1 clockwise, notice that childhood represents Stage I (Hall's model); this is the stage where the leader typology is autocratic moving toward benevolent autocratic, and Stage II is where the more

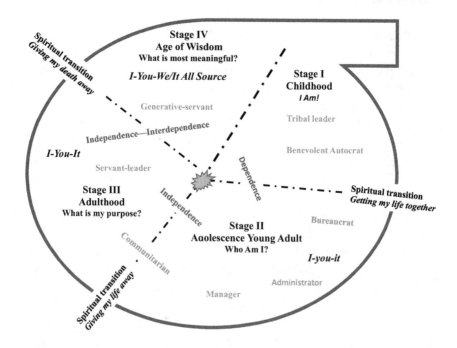

Fig. 2.1 Life stages and leadership development

complex systems call for administrators and managers. Communitarian leadership is depicted partly as a transitional style embracing some Stage II and some Stage III values and skills. Stage III is where more collaborative Servant-leadership comes to fruition. Stage IV reflects the values, skills, and dispositions of the Generative-servant. Note that Servant-leadership as a predominant form of leadership constellates at Stage III and spans Stage III and Stage IV, indicating all leadership typologies regardless of the label (prophetic, visionary, or generative) are a variation of Servant-leadership.

Figure 2.1 also depicts stages of dependence, independence, and *independence–interdependence*; these notations represent the predominate focus of the developmental priority; however, all three variations are at play in each stage. In addition, the previously described *I–You* relational dynamic has been included. On the right-hand side of Fig. 2.1, the *I–You* differentiation is shown at Stage II and prevails in relationships. *I–You* and *We* are presented in Stages III and IV, respectively, depicting a growth in relational awareness and a profound expansion of valuing care and respect for all.

To the right of Stage I, in Fig. 2.1, is the statement *I am*, reflecting the beginning of individuating ego development. At Stage II, *who am I* is most relevant. At Stage III, *what is my purpose* becomes a priority. At Stage IV, *what is most meaningful* becomes the greater priority. Again, all three questions are relevant within each developmental stage; however, each question is most prevalent with the stage it is associated with. These three questions probe and stimulate the human spirit and are relevant to our growth and development. Accompanying each of these three questions is a spiritual movement. The question *who am I* involves the spiritual movements associated with *getting my life together*; this is the initiating spiritual impetus (inspiration) for the shift from Stage I to Stage II. The question *what is my purpose* involves responding to my vocation or call, which initiates the spiritual movements associated with *giving my life away (serving)* our life of work, raising a family, and service to the collectives we support; this is the spiritual impetus for shifting from Stage II to Stage III. And the final question *what is most meaningful* initiates the spiritual movements associated with man's search for ultimate meaning denoted by *giving my death away*, involving developing a transforming mind by loosening our grip on our beloved ideas, our convictions, and our worldview so that we can *live in the here and now—here and now*. Only in consciously learning to die, to let go, can we live in the transforming moment and be of ultimate service as a wise elder; this is the spiritual impetus for shifting from Stage III to Stage IV (Rolheiser, 2014). Variations of these three fundamental human questions and the spiritual movements associated with them drive (in part) the quest for growth and development during our life journey. As each of the four worldviews represents a stage of consciousness, each stage has a particular focus of values associated with it which become a focal point for seven different leadership typologies. Based on this understanding of human development, I presume to make the claim that we are all potentially *Servant-leaders in training*.

Hall (1994) claimed that values are the building blocks of human nature. Values, represented by words (meanings), reflect significant concepts that underlie all human decisions and actions. Values represent internal images or ideals that form the basis for our external behaviors. We actualize our values in our day-to-day activities through the skills we practice. Hall indicated we choose our value priorities as a result of how we view the world and our role in it. As we grow and develop, our value priorities change, become more complex, and our worldview expands. For example, values become more complex as they transition from valuing family belonging to peer support, to empathy, to empowerment. Values that have been integrated become our new foundation values, which we then use as our operating values while we begin to focus on developing even more complex and related values. The process integrates our present values into the more complex and often more numerous values we are currently striving to integrate, while being drawn by even greater more complex future values—this ongoing value dynamic propels development. Growth signifies an expanding perspective and a greater complexity of integrated dispositions, capacities, values, and skills, enacted through the development of instrumental, relational, imaginal, and system skills. Growth implies more than merely understanding, growth implies a practiced shift toward greater application.

Growth, however, is not guaranteed by mere potential or even aging. Inertia seems to keep people in their current stage. Individuals may remain in Stage I, for example, acting on the values of that stage of maturity for their entire lifespan. Transforming growth from one stage to the next involves an adaptive change and requires a positive interpretation of experience, a yearning for greater meaning and understanding (learning) and an act (risk) of the will (spirit) to metaphorically step out into the desert and engage new experiences and interpretations of our perceived reality. A growth (shift) to a new stage requires a creative act, the integration of state experiences, more complex values, and the some creative development in some or all of four kinds of skills. The critical nature of a shift is not mere *understanding*, but more like a cathartic holistic spirit, body, heart, mind shift, a resolving release that is not as much about *seeing new things* as *a new way of seeing*. Transitioning from one stage to the next requires some dissatisfaction (struggle/resistance) with the status quo, some integration of new awareness (state experiences), and some successful yearning and striving for greater awareness and meaning.

Each of the four stages of development has two elemental states, designated simply as A and B (see Table 2.2). The A state involves the way a person reacts to the world, while the B state is the way a person interacts in the world relationally with others. As development progresses, we alternate from a focus on self A to a focus on B learning the values and skills to interact with others within our family, group, organization, community (Beck & Cowan, 2006). Importantly, self-values have to be desired, practiced, and personally integrated to some minimum extent before we are able to authentically model them in the collective. Thus, a person who merely gives lip service to unintegrated values and skills will appear to others as inauthentic and manipulative, or even coercive.

Each stage of development is determined by how the individual responds to three elemental issues and the types of means and goal values a person is attempting to achieve. Elements

- How the world is perceived by the individual?
- How the individual perceives herself/himself functioning in the world?
- What human needs the self seeks to satisfy (Hall, 1994)?

Stage I

In Torbert and Fisher/Rooke model (Table 2.1), Stage I is the domain of the Impulsive and the Opportunist. Metaphorically it is the child's or a survivalist worldview; many adults exist in Stage I, usually because they have grown up in an oppressive environment and have been unable to move on, or because due to environmental circumstances survival has again become the major struggle. The bulk of the history of humanity has lived out their lives within this stage. We first experience leadership from (or as) the autocrat or tyrant. The tyrant claims power: remember the *terrible two's*. Unless we are called forth from our tyranny and have ways of getting what we want positively modeled for us, tyranny will remain our primary style of leadership, or remain the primary one we regress to under stress when the environment is perceived to become uncooperative or hostile.

Stage I is a worldview in which we perceive our self to be struggling to survive; we have a limited view of anything beyond personal physical satisfaction and needs. Adults in Stage I have a worldview characterized by an absence of control and responsibility. They feel they have no (or little) control over their own lives, and that responsibility for their actions is due to external circumstances (powerful others; Gods, parents, bosses, determinism dictators, or institutions). At Stage I the individual seeks to satisfy physical human needs for food, warmth, shelter, and sexual pleasure. Self-preservation and security motivate us to acquire the skills that will guarantee safety and survival. Much of media advertising is directed at this impulsive opportunistic stage with a focus on sensual images for improving appearance and making people feel good.

At Stage I, values are aligned through a centralized hierarchy. In the traditional hierarchical organization, the founder's (cultural) values were expected to be held by everyone who worked in the organization. Employees are expected to be committed to the founder's point of view. Loyalty and commitment means loyalty and commitment to the leadership of the organization. Fear based on survival needs motivated employees to contribute a sufficient amount of their human potential to achieve the mission of the organization.

Autocratic Leadership

Autocratic leadership is hardly ever elected; it is usually appointed out of survival necessity. Autocrats (Table 2.2) assume that major decisions have to be made by the leader; leaders need to keep tight control over their subordinates, that is, a patient in an intensive care unit of a hospital would typically experience autocratic leadership. Control of property, profit margin, and financial flow are of utmost importance, and loyalty to the leader/organization is the number one priority. Autocratic leadership is most essential when the environment is alien, when safety and survival struggles are occurring. For example, if you are in charge of a desert/jungle search team in wartime, your leadership style is most often autocratic. However, when leadership is autocratic in a physically non-threatening environment, it becomes oppressive and demeaning to the membership and is an unhealthy style of leadership for followers and the leader. An autocratic style would then be perceived as over controlling, placing unrealistic expectations on others, and the leader's primary loyalty is to self.

Organizations are traditionally very structured top-down hierarchies where leadership authority is unquestioned. In some environments this is an appropriate structure. We need to assess the values appropriate to the environment and the needs of the people in that situation, then to design the management structure and provide the leadership style that is based on the appropriate environmental or changing situational needs.

Benevolent Paternalist/Maternalist Leadership

The leadership of the benevolent paternalist or maternalist, Stage IB, is one of caring authority; it is autocratic but with an emphasis on care and listening. The leader is very much aware that she or he is ultimately responsible for decisions. Loyalty to designated superiors and following the rules they set down is important. Personal credibility and a resistance to change often mark the leader's style. The leader cares about the employee but would never consider what the employee had to say to be of overriding significance as far as major decision-making is concerned. The follower feels oppressed, but cared for, as a child feels about a parent.

Paternalism was the typical mode of operating for most executives until the late 1960s. Paternalism/maternalism is most appropriate in an environment where the founder of the organization is highly educated and skilled and the support people are not. In this setting, the leader often has to take a parental or teacher role in order for the system to survive. This form of leadership is developmentally destructive when competent educated and trained peers are involved.

The organization at the IB stage is viewed as a family; loyalty is a priority, and dissension is viewed as a personal betrayal. Benevolent hierarchies are managed from the top down, all decisions are made by appointed leadership—often leadership that own or founded the organization. Most (first and second generation) family-owned businesses use this leadership typology. An inherent danger of this kind of leadership is to hire friends and family (rather than competence) into the business. The benevolent organization can very often exaggerate the already dominant cultural roles or stereotypes of men and women in society. In systems where the male leader is a father figure as in religion or sometimes medicine, it is very difficult for women to function and break the stereotype. Likewise, in professions where women are parental role figures, as in teaching and nursing, there is a similar danger of exaggerating and falling into stereotypic roles.

Stage II

In Stage II, we begin to attend to our relationship with other people, family, organizations, and community. We yearn for acceptance and to belong and we develop the skills to succeed with other people. In Torbert and Fisher/Rooke model (Table 2.1), this is primarily the domain of the Diplomat and the expertise of the Technician where relational skills are beginning to develop while the instrumental or professional skills are being refined.

The world is perceived as a problem with which we can cope. We survive and succeed by belonging, conforming, and adapting to the norms of the dominant group, or society, beginning with family. To belong we must learn the value language of the group, how to relate and communicate and play by the rules to demonstrate personal achievement. The most important goal (value) at Stage II and for the rest of our lives is striving for self-worth. Our self-worth is affirmed with the knowledge that people whom we know and respect also respect us. Who am I is an applicable question throughout Stage II, and though we sometimes do not like it much, we are dependent on the approval of others to function within the organizational system. Personal identity emerges from finding our place in the world of work, and in social and religious institutions. This is the stage where the dominant cultural stereotypes of the differences between men and women are most predominant and distinguishable.

The world at Stage II is perceived to be mechanistically ordered, hierarchically driven, and run by the rules of society, and the universe. The laws, when applied, give predictable results that are stable and secure. Currently, most traditional corporate management structures are based on Stage II values such as administration, control, personal achievement, productivity, efficiency, and economic success.

The human needs the self seeks to satisfy are to experience belonging and success, and realize a sense of self-worth. We find meaning less through the satisfaction of the senses and more through the experience of cooperating in a worthwhile enterprise. In Stage II, we value work as productive labor because it provides us with the conviction that we are useful and have earned the right to belong. Because of our need to belong socially, we begin to consider, and even value, the other person's perspective—a step beyond accepting authority. In Stage II, the established order is still pretty much a closed system preserved by law, rules, loyalty, respect, and patriotism. Success is valued as being educated, productive, and achieving.

More decentralized, Stage II (2.0) organizations are market centered emphasizing belonging and achievement needs, where managers attain a greater percentage of their employee's potential through the use of incentives, performance feedback systems, and team building. Management concepts and metrics provide for the measurement of achievement, a sense of accomplishment and the feeling of being part of a work family.

Manager

The leadership priority at IIA is efficient management. Business is seen as ordered and productive, with many expert technicians (Tolbert and Fisher/Rooke model, Table 2.1). The institution is ordered in layers having different functions and levels of power and authority. The system is governed according to the principles of scientific management such as LEAN and a variety of other modern innovative processes. Respect for superiors and the rules and policies of the organization are viewed as being of paramount importance. Institutional authority has replaced parental authority.

Positive learning experiences with institutional leadership are necessary for a person to develop into the later more complex leadership styles—this may entail learning from both positive and negative leadership experiences. This is the last of the autocratic styles, characterized by hierarchical structures that view the system as being made up of leaders and loyal members. Followers experience leadership as considerably less distant than the earlier stages. Leaders at their best are sensitive listeners who take everything that followers say into consideration, as long as it reflects loyalty to the institution and helps make the system more efficient in accomplishing its goals.

The main organizational orientation at IIB is organizational preservation. The organization is the large, efficient, ordered bureaucracy that may be transitioning to an orderly, layered hierarchical market-oriented system. This ordered rational system has been the growing structure of all major institutions—from hospitals to multinational organizations for the last 50 years. For the most part, leaders in these institutions are elected or chosen through the hierarchy itself. The system has formal and informal organizational structures that range from simple to complex.

The system is political and requires loyalty and obedience if it is to function well. In fact, the higher the level of obedience in the system, the more efficient it is. For example, modern corporations focus on the alignment of values and the synchronicity of systems. A negative aspect of this institutional stage is a form of "systems narcissism" that occurs when a system begins to insulate itself against adaptive change.

Communitarian

Beck and Cowan (2006) call this leadership communitarian. This typology straddles Stage IIB and Stage IIIA. Leaders in this transition are enablers and mentors. Communitarians are caught between adherence to the institutions' demands, procedures, and systems versus a new emerging view of human dignity and a renewed sense of self. At this point, the leader/follower distinction is not clear (values are in transition, and are often contradictory). The style is basically that of enabling human interaction through the use of management skills. A laissez-faire form of leadership can develop, with the leader unable to make critical directional decisions if it means disrupting relationships. Interestingly, the perceived negative, indecisive "touchy-feely" weaknesses many practitioners indiscriminately attribute to Servant-leadership more accurately refer to this enabling communitarian leadership. Cynicism arises within this group when there is much talk about shared leadership, equality rights, empowerment, and participation, but abdication of leader responsibility and development is the reality—at the expense of progress.

As a communitarian leader we are often pulled between regressing to our former management style that somehow does not provide meaning anymore versus risking commitment to the responsibilities of and relational demands of collaborative Servant-leadership. The institution often ceases to exist for the communitarian as we attempt to just to be true to ourselves. Developing creative visioning and system planning are important skills to develop at this stage. For example, learning planning skills that can envision the future five to ten years ahead is different from the previous stages that viewed planning as looking one year ahead. Rejuvenating imaginal and creative skills and enhancing one's interpersonal skills are critical for ongoing development at this stage.

Stage III

Stage III emerges when we begin to develop an independent sense of ourselves as separate and distinct from our family and other important groups and individuals. The world becomes a creative project in which we want to participate and to which we have something unique and creative to offer. In the Torbert and Fisher/Rooke model (Table 2.1), this is the domain of the Achiever and the emerging Strategist. We begin to honor our own knowledge and judgment rather than trusting the correctness of the rules and regulations that govern our environment. Stage IIIA values focus on mature independence, personal expressiveness, and development along with a strong yearning for equality and freedom. Authority is viewed as coming from within ourselves, unlike the previous two stages where authority was viewed as external. Stage IIIB values expand our sense of ourselves and the access to power with values that reflect a concern for an institutional and societal level of interdependence. We find meaning in and accept responsibility for revitalizing and even reshaping the environments in which we live, accompanied by a renewed focus on our own creativity integrated with a more expansive and inclusive social conscience.

We find ourselves functioning in the world with an internalized maturity that no longer needs the affirmation of others to realize self-worth, and we no longer find meaning in merely living up to the expectations of others. Creativity and imagination reawakened, along with a newfound sense of honesty (integrity) that makes conformity for its own sake hypocritical. We begin to respect the authority of our own inner voice—the voice that urges us to be congruent and authentic. The personal needs we seek to satisfy are authenticity, meaningful purpose, and the freedom to be creative. We seek independence and integration characterized by a huge shift in our conscience formation. We are able to make self-initiating decisions about what we think is right and wrong without undue reliance on outside authority.

In Stage III, we see ourselves functioning in a world where control and responsibility are chosen and experienced internally. We are able to transcend our own limited worldview and become sensitive to the rights of others. The fact that we have equality and rights for ourselves implies that we need to ensure the rights of others (interdependence) to protect and enhance our own freedom. Ethics and moral values become a greater concern, thus Greenleaf's ethical *test* of Servant-leadership. For the first time, we recognize that there are different points of view on significant issues, and we move toward a rational, objective view of truth and justice that transcends the individual, and the values associated with independence toward a priority for interdependence. Greenleaf's concept of *first among equals* begins to germinate as we come to view leadership as collective endeavor. Individually we become interested in vision and vocation, and value diversity; institutionally we become interested in vision, mission, and principles.

Employees search for greater meaning from their work. The search for more meaning is rooted in a general values shift to Stage III (3.0 Network systems). This shift entails the hierarchy is no longer as singularly essential and effective as it was perceived to be at earlier times, or in hostile, or life threatening environments. Loyalty and obedience can no longer be taken for granted as earlier notions of power are shifting toward influential persuasion. Influence becomes a priority in Stage III and continues as a structural value in the Stage IV.

Servant-Leader

Stage IIIA leadership is facilitative and democratic (Servant-leaders in training). Leaders are often overtly independent, but peer authority is taken seriously (*first among equals*). The leader's seeks value clarity while being energized by enhanced imaginal and system skills. Time management problems and competing priorities create personal stress marking a need to learn to balance work and play. Leaders are enthusiastic and visionary and strive to develop empathy and conflict management skills. Leaders have the ability to enable others to plan ten to twenty years into the future. Organizations at this stage are built on a declared values orientation, which gives equal weight to efficiency and human dignity in the organization. The emerging network structure is open to influence from expertise outside of the organization and human resources become highly valued.

Servant-leadership involves interdependent governance by a peer team—implying that Servant-leadership (*first among equals*) is a collaborative endeavor. Servant-leaders have an informed and growing global perspective and the ability to comprehend how institutional practices are supported and affirmed though the values of each individual person and the systems within the institution. This typology reflects the transition from a focus on independence toward a focus on independence–interdependence. Leaders realize that trust and appropriate intimacy foster team synergy and creativity as they work to create systems that reflect pre-chosen values. Needless to say, Servant-leaders need to be clear about their values or they may misuse their power to the detriment of the organization and society.

Organizations at Stage IIIB value trustworthy leadership. Values are used as criteria for organizational planning, systems creation, and adaptation that strive to maximize the development of all individuals in the system while guarding the efficiency of the organization and attending to the good of society as a whole. The Servant-leader is interested not only in what is produced in the organization but also in the quality of interaction within the organization and the impact of the organization and its products on the quality of life in society. The strategic issue is that leadership is always a team process focused on the institutions capacity to grow, adapt, and learn. There is layered mentoring of leaders, where leaders at higher stages mentor those less experienced. Leadership has a common vision based on core values arrived at by a general consensus. The organization is a system laced with cross-disciplinary teams that are connected through a collaborative communications network.

Stage IV

At Stage IV, the world becomes even more expansive both externally and internally. Without it becomes cosmic and within it becomes infinite. The interdependent *We* responds to the common call to work for global harmony, to care for and renew the earth (servant-stewardship). Actualization of the *independence–interdependence* dynamic affirms that we assume responsibility and at times take the initiative to act independently for the benefit of the team (meso), the community (macro), or the world (mundo). This is the domain of the Strategist and beyond in Torbert and Fisher/Rooke model (Table 2.1).

The world is perceived by the individual at Stage IV as a mystery for which we independently–interdependently care on a global scale. Individually we assume personal and internal disciplines, and external responsibility for the world at large. We perceive ourselves functioning in the world with others to enhance the quality of life. A global care taker consciousness assumes responsibility for initiatives undertaken with other like-minded people.

A key factor for the self is a balance of intimacy and solitude, and the pursuit of congruence and harmony in the whole of creation. Truth and transcendence involve using technology to help the earth to become what it was intended to be naturally. Values are extended into the practical realm internationally as human rights, macroeconomics, and global systems. We see ourselves in contact with the creative life forces that make ecological balance on the planet possible from a scientific point of view. Choices always come from an *all of us*, and a *there I am also* perspective.

At Stage IV the world is viewed as a mystery for which we are responsible stewards. The individual perceives herself/himself to function as a *WE* (*I–You* and *all of us*) to enhance the quality of life. We seek to see things in their wholeness and understand the interrelatedness of the frequently fragmenting parts. The world's present condition needs to be aligned with its natural and future potential—and this requires a capacity of deep generative listening, generative dialog, and pathfinding-foresight. *WE* experience a yearning to improve global harmony through communal action and collaboration. Individually *WE* assume internal control and external responsibility for the world. At Stage IV we exhibit comfortableness with paradox, seeking harmony in the chaos and tension of apparent opposites. The concept of nurturing congruence and harmony applies to the inner life of the individual, as well as to the external world. Inner harmony is to be integrated with social harmony through the use of appropriate acts and technology. Thus, we strive to use our technology to ensure we do not become its victim.

Generative-Servants

The Generative-servant is primarily creative, visionary, prophetic, and transforming. Generative-servants are attuned to flow as a capacity. Flow arises from generative listening, and generative dialog. Attunement to flow helps identify what disrupts flow within ourselves and the groups, systems, organizations, and communities. Generative-servants work with systems of interdependent governance with peer teams of people who manage system based on clarified values. This typology relies on a global systems perspective and an ability to see how a specific institution globally relates to other institutions. Planning can be 50 years, or seven generations, into the future. The values chosen to create organizational flourishing are translated into institutional practices. The practices are then creatively examined and continuously amended to support a transforming integrative perspective throughout the organization. Misuse of power is a great threat to this form of leadership. So far in human history only a small percentage of people have actually got to the Generative-servant stage.

The institutional style is one of international inter-institutional collaboration. The skills at this level require the integration of Stage IV with Stages I, II, and III. Leaders are concerned about global world order at the human and environment levels. The priority is harmony amidst diversity, and the environment, world peace, and human equality are major concerns. Scharmer's 4.0 ecosystems are examples of all source open system structures.

In summary, from this very brief and eclectic introduction to human development, we see that at each subsequent stage of development, we tend to focus on different values priorities, and the inclusivity of our perspectives expands as we progress. Similarly, as we institute our values, the values an organization originally founded itself on may change as time, effort, experience, and human understanding of system efficiencies change (i.e., Scharmer's 1.0, 2.0, 3.0, 4.0 structures, Table 2.2). As with each individual, every organization, and community, has its own unique culture, underpinned by a value system. Organizations that have successfully endured through history have been clear on their values—then and now. Today, a Stage III environment nurtures values such as human dignity, creativity, cooperation, collaboration, and management systems embedded with those chosen values. Such organizations need to develop leaders with the skills to model and institute those values.

1st Tier–2nd Tier Development

Beck and Cowan (2006) described the transition from 1st Tier to 2nd Tier (see Table 2.1) as the most significant transition in adult development. Our interior work on 2nd Tier values and skills eventually involves the full integration of all prior value systems, which up to this point have been relatively exclusive. In other words, autocrats, bureaucrats, the managers, and communitarians have to some extent evolved mutually exclusive value systems. The daunting task for Servant-leaders in training is the integration of these earlier values systems. Integration involves empathy, forgiveness, aware healing, and creative learning within ourselves and for those currently living out the 1st Tier of their development. Integration involves the ability to see the world more holistically (expansively and inclusively) as one matures and to more consistently act in ways congruent with our value priorities.

Hall (1994) indicated there are two major factors in this shift toward integrated consciousness; when a person enters Stage IIB–IIIA, the critical institutions of influence are likely to be the workplace and higher education, and people begin to be more consistent and self-initiating in exercising leadership. As people become self-initiating, they begin to alter the institutions that affect their lives. They begin to create institutional life rather than simply react within it. Consequently, the notion of personal and organizational transformation emerges and this transforming tendency influences our worldview. The transforming inclinations lead to improving and reshaping life in organizational systems and society.

Institutions, schools, and other organizations have a special role in facilitating personal and leadership development. In order for us to continue to grow through the typologies, the institutional influences in our lives need to be supportive, and they need to reinforce our values at levels slightly ahead of our development; this is about intentional supportive systems and leadership modeling. Growth occurs more easily with institutional reinforcement; thus, it is essential to emphasize the leader and the stakeholder roles in organizational and systems design. A lack of intentional supportive leadership risks confusion and chaos, and contradictory priorities, and a lack of congruent modeling may keep a group stuck in a communitarian role with no consistent directional leadership.

Future values pull us forward developmentally. When we are in the communitarian typology (the stage between 1st and 2nd Tiers), the pull becomes even stronger, because our worldview begins to change paradigmatically from this point on. The world becomes significantly more expansive; these changes alter our behavior toward relationships and fundamentally in the way we see and relate to institutions. Our worldview begins to expand with an internal shift in our perception of who runs and directs our lives. Changing from an exterior orientation (parents, church, rules, and laws) toward an inner directedness, we recognize that we have leadership abilities and that we have a unique contribution to influence the world around us. We may recognize a desire to serve-first. Leadership emerges as a team effort and responsibility.

Shifts in values, skills, and our worldview occur as we recognize opportunities for optimum development, especially in the area of organizational redesign and systems reframing. The values shift also requires learning and integrating new skills. The shift begins with a higher level of interpersonal functioning demanded by values like empathy and empowerment; these may in turn stimulate further development of imaginal skills such as gratitude and joy, and the rejuvenation of creativity. Shifting toward greater interdependence influences the development of enhanced system awareness and system skills, with values such as mission, vision, strategy, and new order (Hall, 1994).

Within the communitarian typology, the group and its values become the central reinforcing factor for the exceptional growth of an individual or leader. Importantly, the values of the group tend to determine or demand leadership that reflects the group norms. Because the communitarian typology resides between two worldviews, the way to shift to Stage III is through a clarification of values and supportive skills. If an individual or an organizational shift is to occur, the leadership group's values must be explicit and embedded organizationally. We clarify our value priorities by identifying the contradictions in our worldview. If we remain in denial about the contradictions between Stage II and Stage III, we swim in a leaderless sea of relativism. The personal and leadership work at this stage is to clarify values that create flourishing in Stage III and move toward greater integration, congruence, and harmony. Servant-leadership is a value-based philosophy that acknowledges coherent values that support communitarians becoming Servant-leaders.

Interestingly, 2nd Tier integration of Stage IV development is not so much about moving beyond Stage III, as it is about the holistic integration of Stages I, II, and III. The only way we make peace with the paradoxes of Stages I, II, and III is through IV. As with each of the other stages, Stage IV consciousness does not just happen, we just do not step into that realm and boom we have arrived, we need to develop even more clarified (complex) values and supportive skills. Holistic values such as gratitude, forgiveness, harmony, wisdom, valuing collective intelligence, and global awareness are the personal and interpersonal challenges involved in developing a Stage IV worldview.

Beck and Cowan (2006) suggest that consciousness progresses like waves moving forward, cresting, and receding and then gathering together (integrating and mixing) before a completely new wave surges forward again perhaps exceeding, or not, the advancement of the previous one. In this sense, Stage IV waves of development are emerging globally within humanity, and we need to deliberately, systematically, and interdependently grow Stage IV capacity in ourselves and others. Developing Stage IV capacity is Servant-leader work. Wilber (2017) indicated that approximately five percent of the world population is in or approaching Stage IV. Simultaneous with Stage IV development is the development of a Stage IV worldview, a (cosmic) global systems perspective. Developing a servant-consciousness is part of the cresting wave serving the greater development of the transition into Stage IV.

The values and skills associated with each typology are well documented in Beck and Cowan (2006) and Hall (1994). This presentation is focused primarily on those values deemed most pertinent to Servant-leader development. The focus on the specific values emphasized herein is not comprehensive; there are certainly other values influential to Servant-leader development.

References

Beck, D. E., & Cowan, C. C. (2006). *Spiral dynamics: Mastering values, leadership, and change*. Malden, MA: Blackwell.

Hall, B. P. (1994). *Values shift: A guide to personal & organizational transformation*. Rockport, MA: Twin Lights.

Kegan, R., & Lahey, L. L. (Eds.). (2009). *Immunity to change*. Boston, MA: Harvard Business Press.

Morelli, M. D., & Morelli, E. A. (Eds.). (2002). *The Lonergan reader.* Toronto: University of Toronto Press.

Prosser, S. (2010). *Servant leadership: More philosophy, less theory.* Westfield, IN: Greenleaf Center.

Rolheiser, R. (2014). *Sacred fire: A vision for deeper human and Christian maturity.* New York: Image.

Scharmer, O., & Kaufer, K. (2013). *Leading from the emerging future: From ego-system to eco-system economies.* San Francisco: Barrett-Koehler.

Wilber, K. (2006). *Integral spirituality: A startling new role for religion in the modern world.* Boston, MA: Integral Books.

Wilber, K. (2017). *Trump and a post truth world.* Retrieved November 2016 from https://www.google.ca/search?q=trump+and+a+post-truth+world+ken+wilber&oq=Trump+and+a+post&aqs=chrome.0.0j69i57j0l4.8025j0j7&sourceid=chrome&ie=UTF-8

3

Leadership Development

Leadership and Values Development

About 2400 years ago, Plato, the classic idealist, mused about the ideal kind of leadership for a *well-governed city*.

> If you discover a life better than ruling for those who are going to rule, it is possible that your well-governed city will come into being. For here alone will the really rich rule, rich not in gold but in those riches required by the happy man, rich in a good and prudent life. (Plato, Blooms Trans., 1968, Book VII/521 a)

Plato's musings suggest that leaders should be motivated by something other than gold or a desire to rule and posed that the only people suited to such a role were philosopher kings. Philosopher kings were people in ancient, and perhaps modern, times who valued and honored the "idea of the good...as all that is right and fair in everything" (Book VII/517 c) and believed that "what was just" held the greatest value for serving and fostering the city (Book VII /540 d–e) or the community or the organization. Plato's words still seem to have a ring of rightness and wisdom about

© The Author(s) 2018
J. H. Horsman, *Servant-Leaders in Training*,
Palgrave Studies in Workplace Spirituality and Fulfillment,
https://doi.org/10.1007/978-3-319-92961-3_3

them, as they awaken hope for our future, calling for mature leaders who are holistic and integrated. Greenleaf's philosophy, similar in some respects to Plato's, holds that serving is better than ruling.

As referred to earlier, it is critical that our understanding of leadership is not oversimplified by ignoring the essential basics of leadership developmental in the context of human development. Each leadership typology suits a particular environment and set of circumstances that make it effective, that is, command and control often suits the circumstances in combat, emergency, and survival situations. I suspect, however, that a person with Stage III or IV values and skills cannot regress to command and control, and persist there long term and remain in harmony with oneself and others. So, a complex form of situational leadership must come into play (to be described). Each of the four stages of development reflects a distinct worldview while also reflecting types of leadership. Leadership development assumes that each leadership typology has reciprocal effects on the follower's experience as each particular expression of leadership is rooted in a set of values that influence our perception of how organizational members are viewed and experienced. The first four leadership typologies are variations of autocratic leadership and are all characterized by a leader–follower format in which management governs normally through carefully designed hierarchical structures crafted for control and efficient institutional functioning.

The transitionary shift to a Stage III worldview, described by Hall (1994) as *enabling*, is an in-between mentoring somewhat therapeutic transition that seems to have evolved into a more developed Communitarian value system (Beck & Cowan, 2006). Stage IIIA is about establishing a mature independence while working to learn the values and skills associated with comprehending and practicing *independence–interdependence*. Once a person embraces the awareness that serving-first is the way to greater integrated wholeness, and assumes the role of a Servant-leader in training, serving becomes the context for leading from that point forward. Stage IIIB involves greater integration of cognitive intelligence, emotional intelligence, spiritual intelligence, and moral intelligence. As our worldview changes, we begin to see everything from a creative perspective. Creativity, a catalyst for integration, emerges from knowing our knowledge is limited, and when put to the test rather than opting for more control, a Servant-leader's automatic response is to listen and build relationships even if that sometimes means erring on the side of trust, compassion, and generosity when calling forth others.

Advancing to Stage IV involves an even more profound reintegration back to our origins (Stages I–III) revisiting unresolved issues experienced during the earlier stages of development. Jaworski (2012) described Stage IV leaders as *Renewing Leaders*: "Stage IV leaders embody the characteristics and values of servant leaders but have matured to a more comprehensive and subtle level of development. They exhibit a capacity for extraordinary functioning and performance" (p. 55). While agreeing with Jaworski's description of leaders at Stage IV, the name *Renewing Leader* does not seem to capture the generative nature and engagement of this kind of leadership, nor acknowledge the servant-first emphasis, thus the name *Generative-servants*. A Generative-servant is profoundly relational, creative, holistic, and integrative. The generative term is an outgrowth of an integration of body, mind, heart, and spirit and a renewed creative capacity based on generative listening and generative dialog, a capacity that acknowledges, affirms, and nurtures individual and community actualization, development, and flourishing.

Some developmentalists indicate that organizational members will not understand (relate with) a leader who is more than one (or a 1/2) typology ahead of the membership (Zohar & Marshall, 2004; Beck & Cowan, 2006). Accordingly, it is understandable, and worthy of empathy and compassion, that organizational members find it difficult to comprehend—let alone be motivated about Servant-leading when followers are functioning as autocrat (preservers) or even communitarians (sensitive searchers). If we are to call forth those we lead, the most effective value language to use is that a half stage ahead of the individual or the group. For example, a Servant-leader may choose to behave as a maternalist leader to call forth followers who are oppressed; the leader relates values from IIA because that is where the IB person (group) needs them to be (calling them forth with a value language they can relate to); nevertheless, the IIA leadership behavior is done with a Servant-leader (IIIB) consciousness; the Servant-leader can be authentic because she has integrated IB and IIA values. This insightfully adaptive form of situational leadership emerges from prior value integration, from understanding and empathy, and from placing a priority on empowerment. It is a form of situational leadership that is not intentionally coercive or manipulative, although it may appear that way to some.

For example, in the context of rapidly deteriorating environments, the challenge for the Servant-leader is to maintain her values and skills aware-ness even as she shifts into an IB command and control mode to deal with a particular issue. Importantly, the leader needs the awareness not to remain in IB once the threat has passed and the environment is no longer hostile, as that leader will be experienced by the group members as oppressive once the hostilities are over. In changing environments (from combat to peace, or from code blue emergencies to stable), the task for a Servant-leader is to provide the appropriate leadership for the emergency and, for the aftermath, to ensure members transcend back through the stages to their normal/preferred mode of functioning. The transition may occur in a matter of minutes, or it may take months, or even years depending on the situation. Group members who previously functioned at the collaborative level will yearn to return to that value system if the environment is conducive—anything less will be experienced as oppres-sive. Again, these situations call for an understanding of this situational (spiral dynamic) leadership (Beck & Cowan, 2006). Importantly, the focus is not only on the well-being of the individuals and the group, it is also on the well-being of the organization and the overall system.

Another point on leadership, if an organization wants to practice Servant-leadership, it must have leaders with a relational values orienta-tion for that to occur. We cannot apply higher-level relational values (dynamic situational leadership) without those integrated values and a more expansive vision of influential responsibility. The leadership group (at least) needs the integrated skills and values in order to authentically model and systematize the values that they profess and model. Servant-leaders strive to help those they lead learn the value language of the group. Lip service, however, without the authentic modeling and the systems change that support the values is manipulative and will create distrust and cynicism.

What about followers? It is important to understand that the concept of "subordinates" or "followers" is itself a judgment/perspective that occurs primarily in Stages I and II, although there seems to be some cultural carry over to the higher stages. It is a perception by leadership of the membership, and a reciprocal view of leadership by the followers. It is a description of how each perceives and behaves toward the other by virtue of their understanding of reality—their worldview. Leadership and membership are bound together symbolically as a whole; they are, in fact, dependent on each other. It is interesting to note that leadership and followership relate to each other differently within each stage. This is why Greenleaf's description of *first among equals*, a Stage III–IV value, is not well comprehended or embraced by those at earlier stages.

Needless to say, in Stage III the changes being called for do not stop at the leader, our role as follower changes as well. The ongoing changes in organizational structure, systems design, and the rise of information technology have increased the need for employee participation and self-direction. The organizational network and ecosystem structures that we are now evolving toward emphasize that rank means expanded responsibility (not more power), where our leadership role is not to command but to call forth and to influence, persuade, and support. Not surprisingly, as with the leader's role, the follower's role requires a similar development shift—to the extent that followers also require self-examination and growth as employee responsibility becomes more complex and more expansive.

The need to authentically influence and persuade rather than command and control denotes a fundamental values shift that provides insight into the kind of humble respect and self-examination leaders and followers need to undergo. A requisite to successful organizational transformation is the need for leaders and followers to first transform themselves through self-examination and interior growth. Prior to effective and lasting organizational structural changes, there is first a need for leadership-follower development. A need for leadership development that no longer distinguishes leaders from followers as superiors and subordinates, but rather assumes we are all leaders and followers.

Additionally, it is very important to be aware that each successive stage is built on the earlier stages, which remain to some extent foundationally intact while consciousness integrates or subsumes previous values. For example, while working on IIIB values such as integration and wholeness, we may also be redressing the value of self-preservation from IB in a new way, as we take on a new job or pursue a new vocation. The paradigmatic shift creates an awareness where one understands and integrates the previous perspective in a new and more holistic way; these integrative shifts may occur gradually, or through crisis, or epiphany experiences.

Servant-Leader Development

To further our understanding of individual growth and leadership development, we need a more complex model. A more elaborate pictorial figure is helpful for conveying, grasping, and interpreting these more complex ideas. To create a three-dimensional figure, let us return to Fig. 2.1 (Chap. 2) and imagine turning the circle (like a coin) on its edge and then with a gentle twisting pull from both ends and we get Fig. 3.1. This is a more complex depiction of the same metaphorical model that now looks like a spiraling shell beginning at the left-hand side with an individual's birth, or emergence, and spiraling horizontally to the right

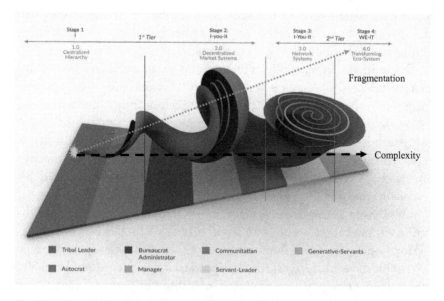

Fig. 3.1 Human development and leadership development. Printed with permission of Gonzaga University

depicting an individual's potential stages of expansion and growth. The spiral depicts the surging, cresting, and receding twists of life and leadership development and shows that life is more than linear sequence of aging, but also expansionary and multifaceted. Figure 3.1 is a pectoral metaphor of potential individual development; it is a depiction based on an understanding of the developmental models that shows evolving development for individuals, leaders, and organizational structures up to Stage IV development as described in the first two chapters.

Figure 3.1 depicts the 1st and 2nd Tiers of four stages of development, each with a focus on I, I–You–It, and We/It. Stage I manifests the centralized hierarchy, Stage II reflects the market system, Stage III reflects network systems, and Stage IV reflects ecosystems. Each of the seven shades of color on the trapezoid bed reflects a leader typology, beginning on the left with Tribal Leader, Autocrat, Bureaucrat/Administrator, Manager, Communitarian, Servant-leader, and ending on the extreme right with Generative-servant. As individuals grow and culture and systems progress, complexity increases along with fragmentation.

Figure 3.1 depicts I, I–You–It, I–You, and We/It as the journey from egocentricity, through ethno-centricity, to global-centricity, to cosmic-centricity. The four developmental stages run horizontally from birth (left) to mature elder hood (right) and are differentiated by three spiritual (vertical) boundaries. These vertical lines represent Rolheiser's spiritual transitions (also see Table 2.1, Chap. 2) marking differentiated expansions of consciousness or worldviews supported by developed values and skills. Rolheiser's spiritual transitions bridge the spiritual enlightenments of *mind, heart, body*, and *being* (Delman, 2018) and, respectively, initiate each of the stages of development. If not inhibited, these spiritual enlightenments continuously inspire holistic integration through each ensuing developmental stage. Developmentally we experience the dawning of mindfulness in Stage I. Transitioning to Stage II (getting our life together) adds the dawning of relational heartfulness. Transitioning to Stage III (giving our life away) adds the dawning of bodyfulness. The transition to Stage IV (giving our death away) initiates the holistic integration of beingfulness. When the mind and the heart are not integrated, our value systems become bi-polarized, evidenced by incongruence in ourselves, in our organizations, and society. Similarly, but more disruptively, when the mind, the heart, and the body are not holistically integrated, the three spiritual enlightenments remain fragmented in tri-polar value systems, revealing even more incongruences. The result is fragmented *being*, and correspondingly more complex fragmented systems, organizations, and society. Much of the incongruence we are experiencing in our era is rooted in these spiritual fragmentations. Figure 3.1 also identifies 1st Tier and 2nd Tier stages of development; Stages I and II are labeled 1st Tier where leadership is generally about personal and organizational power, whereas Stages III and IV, labeled 2nd Tier, reflect the developing influence of serving-first.

What the spiraling image shows is that growth and shifts between stages become more incrementally expansive as we progress developmentally (from left to right horizontally). Additionally, horizontal integration occurs as we gain knowledge, experience, and our values and skills become more numerous and complex. The spiral depicts increasing breadth and complexity (diagonal arrow) as well as a tendency for fragmentation as specialization and consciousness develop (diagonal arrow). As the individual develops, values become complex constructs, yet more clearly differentiated, but not necessarily more numerous.

Below the spiral is a shaded trapezoid that reflects leader typologies (the varying shades of gray reflect Beck and Cowan's (2006) color coded model). The leadership typologies run horizontally from the left to right depicting growth and the integration of values and skills in leadership development as suggested by the spiraling growth of the diagram. The left portion of the trapezoid reflects a greater portion of humanity, which decreases as the stages develop to the right. At the origin (left) of the spiral, we see a star depicting birth, embodiment, integrating insight, and the dawn of understanding. Note the two lines, one dark the other light, running from birth through the center of the spiral horizontally to the bell, where they reveal a galaxy spiral formation. The dark line depicts the personal A stage of development and the light line depicts the relational B stage of development. Together the two lines represent the integrating nature of development. Each shift to a new stage of development requires progressively more integration back through the stages as our identity and consciousness reintegrates new awareness, values, and skills. The point is, no matter what stage we are at, we are never separated from the earlier stages; they remain within us integrating as we heal and learn.

Figure 3.1 also depicts the integrative process occurring horizontally at Stage III. Stage III is not fully enclosed into the spiral, as most of us are still evolving Stage III in our developmental journey, and Stage IV is at a relatively early creational stage for most of the global population. Where the trapezoid represents the bulk of humanity from a current collective and historical perspective, the depiction of a partial but not completed spiral at Stage III and early emerging Stage IV shows that the many individuals have not yet reached the tipping point to complete Stage III development. I suspect this has to do with integrating and systematizing more relational values with the former Stage II and Stage I value systems. For this to occur, it is critical at Stage III and beyond to consciously re-stimulate our creative imaginative capacity.

Regenerating our creative capacity is called for if we are to stimulate 2nd Tier integrated consciousness development. Out of this renewed creativity we can begin to learn to listen and discern more holistically and we can draw into consciousness our capacity for pathfinding-foresight as we learn to draw more of our intelligibility making and sensory capacities into our awareness. Acknowledging, affirming, and stimulating creativity affirms our being and aides the search for renewed meaning and purpose. When creativity becomes part of our conscious disposition, we experience a joyous gratitude for the many gifts of life. New energy flows out of these new insights; energy that if not used creatively will dissipate. The awakening of our imaginal creative energy is requisite for Stage IV development.

Enhanced awareness is an ongoing pursuit of the Servant-leader in training. Wilber (2006) describes the formation of a new worldview (a stage shift) as the concretizing of our states of awareness into a new foundational stage of development. Conscious knowing begins with enhanced awareness, "…enhanced awareness enables greater perception of our sensory experience and other signals from the environment. When one is aware, there is more than the usual alertness, more intense contact with the immediate situation…" (Greenleaf, 1977, p. 27). Greenleaf suggested that attending to awareness involves learning to tap into an inner solitude with whomever, wherever, and whenever we choose. Accessing inner solitude is a state capacity to generatively listening interiorly; this kind of listening makes room for perception of how things are, and that can be disturbing. "Awareness is not a giver of solace-it is just the opposite. It is a disturber and an awakener. Able leaders are usually sharply awake and reasonably disturbed" (Greenleaf, 1977, p. 28). This leads to the notion that inner awareness begets exterior awareness, and vice versa.

Attending to our senses involves intentionally becoming more aware of what we are sensing. Where cognitive multitasking seems to fragment our attention, attending to our organic sensory awareness seems to increase our functional capacity to notice information more holistically, and perhaps realistically. The physicist Moshe Feldenkrais, who developed *awareness through movement* learning, addressed this holistic self-awareness capacity as a new stage in human evolution:

> ...awareness gives us the capacity for judgement, differentiation, generalization, the capacity for abstract thought, imagination, and much more. Awareness of our organic drives is the basis for man's self-knowledge. Awareness of the relationship between these impulses and their origin in the formation of human culture offers man the potential means to direct his life, which few people have yet realized. (Feldenkrais, 1977, pp. 47–48)

Feldenkrais was not referring solely to a rational cognitive capacity but rather a holistic integration that occurs when we *come to our senses*. As our cognitive and rhythmic heart-mind-body system becomes more consciously integrated, we develop a capacity for enhanced awareness that can be experienced as holistic knowing. Servant-leaders in training strive for enhanced awareness by intentionally stimulating their imaginal creativity and learning to listen deeply and in a way that nurtures their capacity for pathfinding-foresight. Stage III and IV development involves being present and available to whatever we are experiencing and that involves both horizontal and vertical integrations.

Horizontal Development and Vertical Integration

Figure 3.2 shows horizontal time as linear and sequential through which we live our life. Vertical (spatial) state experiences enhance awareness and learning. State experiences occur at all developmental stages and may occur when we are awake, asleep, or dreaming. Other metaphorical examples of states are first-person state experiences that occur within the

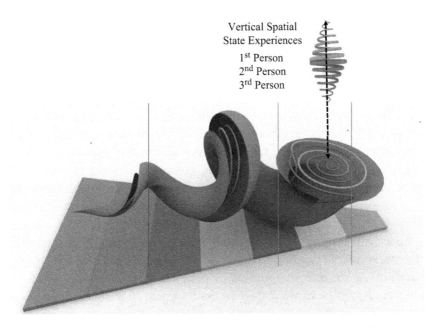

Vertical Spatial
State Experiences
1st Person
2nd Person
3rd Person

Fig. 3.2 Horizontal development and vertical integration. Printed with permission of Gonzaga University

self, relational second-person state experience, and third-person state experiences that occur with others, nature, things, the environment, culture, and history. An accumulation of state experiences may concretize to form a new foundation for a new more expansive integrated stage of development.

In Fig. 3.2, Stages I through IV depict the horizontal time plane, the temporal plane of life experience, where we carry the past, experience the present, and struggle to foresee and adapt to the future; this is the plane where we are put to the test, where we struggle to integrate our focus values and skills. The individual in early development is primarily egocentric with concerns for developing instrumental, safety, and family security-oriented skills. A Stage I individual is for the most part dependent on others and the unpredictability of the environment. Nonetheless, history reveals that some very wise men and women and some great Servant-leaders emerged from Stage I many times and may continue to emerge from this stage. How might we explain Servant-leadership occurrences at Stage I?

St. Benedict's 1500-year-old *Rule* is a great example as it is a very old policy manual for organizing and leading. The *Rule* is still in use as an organizational manual for leading and living in monasteries and a variety of other organizations. The *Rule* is clearly written in an autocratic Stage I hierarchal tone. Nonetheless, when the *Rule* is interpreted in light of Stage III or Stage IV values, serving-first value priorities can be clearly identified. A simple explanation is that St. Benedict, a wise elder, consciously or unconsciously, chose to serve and to live according to the values that serving calls forth—regardless of the stage or the environmental conditions. Wilber (2006) addressed this issue with his explanation of states of consciousness. States are different from stages of consciousness. "Everybody experiences various states of consciousness, and these states often provide profound motivation, meaning, and drives…" (p. 4). States of consciousness (experience) occur on the vertical plane, which simply means that states of consciousness are potentially available to everyone at any time regardless of what stage of development they are at. From state experiences, we gain insights and frequently enhance and modify our awareness and understanding. State experiences may occur while awake, dreaming, or sleeping. They involve spiritual, cognitive, emotional, and physical experiences. Potentially, a full array of human states is available to each person, even though some individuals may experience qualitatively and quantitatively more of these states than others, that is, through contemplation, mystical experiences, dreams, or physical experiences.

Referring back to Fig. 3.2 and examining the bell (right side), Wilber's notions of states of consciousness are depicted as occurring vertically on the face of the horizontal bell of the spiral. State experiences may be personal (dark spiral) and relational awareness (light spiral) and learning. Wilber described state experiences as metaphors of body, mind, spirit; or beauty, goodness, and truth; or 1st person, 2nd person, 3rd person. State experience involve awareness, learning, growth, and integration. Accumulated state experiences are natural and essential for stage development.

Wilber (2006) emphasizes that a person who has had profound, religious, spiritual, or meditative state experiences will interpret those experiences using the value framework of the stage of development they are at (p. 91). Thus, a person immersed in a Stage I culture may have increasingly influential state experiences on the vertical plane; however, they will interpret and articulate their insights and experience using a Stage I worldview. This is simply because they know no other value system. A person in Stage I cannot use a Stage II value system to interpret their experience as they have not integrated that framework of values. Thus, the 1500-year-old experiences and writings of St. Benedict, for example, may have been a highly advanced depiction of values to aspire to (such as respect, flexibility, and compassion); however, the experience was interpreted and articulated according to the horizontal value system of Stage I, and that made sense to the general populace of the time. Similarly, people in Stage II can only explain their experiences using a Stage II value system because that is the framework they are most familiar with.

So why has the *Rule of Benedict* endured for 1500 years? Even though the *Rule* is written in a Stage I language of values, those values remain foundational and are transcendent in that they can be interpreted or reinterpreted through translation and in light of the values of any of the more expanded developmental stages. Recall that the essence of a value does not disappear with integration—it remains foundational as it transforms into more complex interpretations and manifestations. So, just because the *Rule* was written in the tone of a Stage I value system, that does not necessarily mean that for monasteries (or other organizations) to flourish they have to maintain Stage I values. Rather, wise interpretation and adaptation of the *Rule* through, for example, Stage II or Stage III values reveal, expand, and affirm the inherent core values imbedded in the *Rule*. This is why some ancient writings are referred to as wisdom literature. Not only are we able to identify and interpret wisdom literature through various states of consciousness but also from different more expansive stages of development. This suggests a person in Stage III should be able to reflect on a Stage I experience and interpret the meaning using integrated understanding and experience. This may be one of the reasons the *Rule* (Bible, Koran, or Upanishads) endures and still has much to teach us about living in community.

For another example, consider the play, or film *The Lion King*, it is obvious that a benevolent autocracy creates more harmony among the animals than tyranny and chaos—even in very hostile survivalist environments. The enduring truths of this primarily Stage I story may be interpreted with greater meaning through the lens of each of the other expanded stages. Thus, a person from a Stage II or III value framework may discover enduring truths in *The Lion King* that inform and affirm her/his value system. Our values become integrated and more complex as we develop; values such as self-preservation transcend; security influences the need for family belonging, which in turn supports a sense of self-worth competence and confidence, and a sense of self-actualization, which in turn leads to a desire for social and collective actualization based on principles that support global harmony. Thus, a Stage I desire for self-preservation may eventually lead to a desire (with much greater differentiation, integration, understanding, and complexity) for global harmony at Stage IV. At each stage of development, we can be aware of the disharmony (disruptions); at Stage IV we learn to not only sense, feel, and conceptualize the disharmony internally and externally, we also assume responsibility individually and collectively for healing and re-harmonizing the system: this is a more complex view of harmony than what is yearned for within Stage I.

Individual Versus Group Development

The spiral in Figs. 3.1 and 3.2 depicts individual development, whereas group development is quite different (see Chap. 1, Fig. 1.1). Groups do not follow the individual's invariable sequence of development. There are no invariant sequential stages of development for groups, teams, or collectives (Wilber, 2006, p. 151). Collectives refer to families, groups, communities, and societies. Collectives manifest the articulated value systems of its membership. Variations of the familiar patterns of the group development such as forming, norming, storming, performing, and reforming may occur at every stage of developmental. An individual might join a collective at whatever developmental stage the collective manifests. The way one becomes a member of a collective is by learning to communicate and function within the collective value and language system.

A leadership group may call forth members of the organization to transcend their personal development by the way they act and cooperate together in the pursuit of the values embedded in an organizational mission. In other words, if the dominant group is working together to enact a vision that holds Stage III values, organizational members individually at Stage I or II may transcend to that level by enacting those values and learning the associated value language. If members cannot learn the value language of the group, they likely will not remain there. What most effectively calls forth the members is a congruent Servant-leader disposition communicated through word relating and modeling. Consequently, developmental education is necessary for Servant-leaders to learn the appropriate instrumental, relational, system, and imaginal skills to conceptualize reality and articulate their perspectives.

An individual's progress or regression within a collective depends on the value and language system of the leadership group. The central mode of communication focuses on group values and norms. Groups form sometimes for survival reasons; at other times collectives are simply a more comfortable preference. Using leader typologies for groups, autocrats, bureaucrats, managers, and communitarians usually hang out with their own types, simply to be on a comfortable wavelength.

What is obvious to our experience, but seldom stated, is that once a society has developed to a particular value system (i.e., Manager, see Fig. 3.1), collectives in that society do not have to repeat each developmental stage—even though individuals do. For example, Western society is predominantly Managerial. This (generally) means individuals born into Western society must develop from Tribal to Autocrat to Bureaucrat/Administrator to a Managerial capacity, if they are to be successful. Collectives, however, in this society can be formed at any of those four levels, as well as some levels beyond Manager. In other words, a Managerial society is likely to manifest Tribal, Autocratic, and Bureaucrat/Administrator groups along with developing (evolving) Communitarian and Servant-leader collectives, however the majority of the collectives in the society will be Managerial.

Even more interesting is that groups, as well as individuals within a society, can jump levels if the value system of the dominant individuals changes; in other words, an Autocratic collective could become a Managerial collective, or a Bureaucratic/Administrator collective could become Communitarian, if the dominant values and language of the leadership changes. This may explain why a flourishing progressive Servant-leader organization can deteriorate so rapidly when an Autocratic leader is put in charge. Again, sequential development is not necessary for groups. Individual can be in any group, regardless of their stage of development, as long as they can learn the value language and function within that group.

There are at least four implications for community formation that Servant-leaders in training might heed. First, each color group in Stages I and II (1st Tier) has an intact value system and a language of discourse that is to some extent mutually exclusive. So, as stated earlier when leaders speak to individuals, they need to speak in their value (color) language. To call an individual forth to a higher (color) group, a successful leader will begin by articulating values no more than one color higher; otherwise, the leader may not be understood. Servant-leaders thus need to develop an integrated sense of a dynamic form of situational leadership. When dealing with the collective, it is easy to see how complex leadership may become. Attaining and maintaining resonance within a group, an organization, or a community is challenging. When interacting with groups, the leader needs to be respectful, authentic, and responsible just to hold the groups' attention and hopefully their respect. Successful leadership involves learning sophisticated listening skills and an ability to speak to the different values systems among multiple groups, while also articulating the dominant value language of the collective. For those who do not buy in, there are other options; through self-selection or forced selection, they may seek another group whose value language they resonate with.

Second, because the dominant value language can be switched to any color, depending on the value system of the leadership group, it is very important that leadership recruitment efforts are clear about the current group's value system (color) and find leaders who will not alienate organizational members by being too distant (higher or lower) from the current group. Third, the dominant value language can become oppressive under certain circumstances for individuals and/or the group. The solution is not to regress and try to recapture a more comfortable lower imagined past—where this oppression supposedly did not exist, but to move toward a higher value system of increasing care and compassion (Wilber, 2006, p. 150).

Finally, the three previous points call for integrated leaders who have grown (or are open to growing) through each of the stages, and who can relate with individuals, and with groups, at any level with empathy and a capacity to resonate with them wherever they are developmentally. The task set before the Servant-leader in training is to articulate a dominant value system for groups at the highest level most people can resonate with. In other words, the task is not to get everyone into Stage IV—that will never happen. Statistically and developmentally, the majority of the people will be in Stage I or II—this is because individually we cannot avoid the sequential development process. The Servant-leader needs to focus on the health of the entire spiral (individual and collective system). The great challenge for Servant-leaders is to envision and create healthy systems for both individuals and the collective so humans may flourish at all levels of human development.

As mentioned earlier, the stages of development are not as linear as they appear. We all (most healthy people) have access to all four stages, all of the time. Some people may have the capacity to flip from Stage II to Stage III or even Stage IV for a short time; however, they may never get Servant-leadership even though they may be attracted to it. Some have become really good at faking it. Unless the stage's appropriate values and skills are developed, practiced, and integrated, Servant-leadership at best is a training experience, at worst it is just lip service, and that lip service actually augments a lot of distrust and doubt. Those who may tend to see themselves as Stage III or Stage IV elites are very likely still in the 1st Tier of development—with little humility.

Integrative thinking at Stages III and IV seeks a systems view, a global worldview that is consistent with the capacities values and perspectives of Servant-leadership. Inherent with the notions of development is the assumption that greater human flourishing does not occur from regressing. Once we have developed beyond the 1st Tier, we cannot regress to our family of origin community and experience it the way it was, no matter how good we now perceive it to have been, for we have evolved. We can be there in that environment, but we will be there functioning with a different configuration of values. Neither can we regress to one big happy corporate family nor re-create the experience of being on a winning (productive) team. We can only live from the freely chosen set of universal human values, together with others, working toward a flourishing global community.

A collective that does not attempt to be a closed system (a group of elites, a separate society) thrives on striving to be a relatively stable open system in perpetual transformation. A system that is willing to hold the pain and toxicity of humanities paradoxes can nurture the capacity to work with a diversity of key stakeholders fostering greater human harmony. A diverse flourishing collective system may, out of its abundance, support and respectfully serve other sub-groups, to build up our global society. More importantly, these collectives also support individuals regardless of where they are developmentally: this is a responsibility of Servant-leadership.

Leadership Skills

A consequence of studying values is the discovery of a myriad of associated skills. Hall (1994) cataloged 125 universal human values and from those values identified four categories of skills that interact to influence one's transcendence from one stage of consciousness to another (depicted in Fig. 3.3). The skills are listed in the sequential order of their ongoing development. That being said Fig. 3.3 shows that imagining skills are essential for the development of all the skills.

When a full range of skills is not developed in the imaginal, instrumental, relational, and system skills areas, an individual's growth is impeded. When the skills develop in an unintegrated or incomplete way, unconscious moral or destructive decision-making often occurs. When leaders continuously make destructive decisions, there is usually an absence or deficiency in one of the skill areas. For example, without instrumental skills the leader is perceived as incompetent. Insufficient interpersonal relational skills may be the reason a person unconsciously uses the system against others, and cause interminable emotional problems with people.

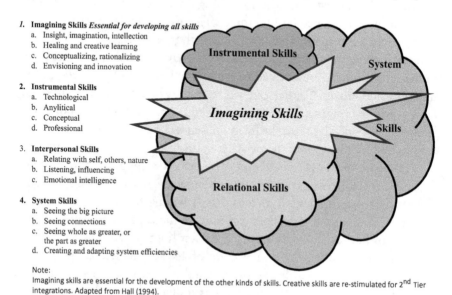

1. **Imagining Skills** *Essential for developing all skills*
   a. Insight, imagination, intellection
   b. Healing and creative learning
   c. Conceptualizing, rationalizing
   d. Envisioning and innovation

2. Instrumental Skills
   a. Technological
   b. Anylitical
   c. Conceptual
   d. Professional

3. **Interpersonal Skills**
   a. Relating with self, others, nature
   b. Listening, influencing
   c. Emotional intelligence

4. System Skills
   a. Seeing the big picture
   b. Seeing connections
   c. Seeing whole as greater, or
      the part as greater
   d. Creating and adapting system efficiencies

Note:
Imagining skills are essential for the development of the other kinds of skills. Creative skills are re-stimulated for 2nd Tier integrations. Adapted from Hall (1994).

Fig. 3.3 Imagining in skill development

Without interpersonal skills, the leader is insensitive. Without systems skills, the leader lacks the ability to deal with complexity, vision, and fragmentation. A lack of systems skills is particularly a problem in large complex organizations, communities, and international settings where people become increasingly distressed, burned out, and leave. A lack of imaginal skills would disenable leaders to take creative risks, and those leaders will attempt to control operations in a more rigid manner. Without imaginal skills, the leader lacks vision and the ability to take risks. The development of these four kinds of skills is essential to the development of Servant-leaders.

What is important to understand from Fig. 3.3 is that imaginal skills are absolutely necessary for the development of instrumental, relational, and system skills; more importantly imaginal skills are essential for the ongoing development of healing and creative learning. Imaginal skills are the driver for human skill development and thus essential developmental stage shifts. A creative capacity is necessary at each stage of our development if the requisite integration process is to occur. An imaginative creativity capacity helps us sort through the ambiguity and paradox and orchestrate the integration need for a successful stage shift. Tier Two integrations involve a heightened imaginal integration involving enhanced spiritual, emotional, physical, and intellectual awareness. The key to stimulating the development of all the skills is the stimulation of the imagining skills. Learning holistic listening and practicing the healing and creative learning are two ways to stimulate the imaginal skills.

Multiple Intelligences

The four developmental skills and the development of a variety of intelligences are interrelated. Why do some leaders seem to be very developmentally advanced in cognitive intelligence, or spiritual intelligence, but less developed in other areas such as emotional intelligence, or moral intelligence? Some recent scandals reveal corporate and political leaders who seem to fit into these profiles. Wilber's (2006) integral model addresses this in terms of what he calls line intelligences. Developmental lines distinguish the human capacity for multiple intelligences. Line intelligences potentially run horizontally through each stage of development. Wilber (2006) suggests there are perhaps a dozen identified intelligences (intelligences are not depicted in figures). Lines of intelligence become more clearly differentiated as complexity expands, broadens, and heightens through the developing stages. The stages of moral development as outlined by Kohlberg (Chap. 1, Table 1.1) are a line intelligence inherent to the spiral.

Interestingly, lines of intelligence do not necessarily unfold together as a group, but seem to develop individually with some interrelated stimulus from other lines. For example, cognitive intelligence is a primary influencer of other developing lines of intelligences, but it does not necessarily drive the other intelligence lines, other factors are involved. Research indicates that each individual seems to have one to three lines that they are advancing; for example, a person may have developed cognitive intelligence to Stage III, emotional and moral intelligence to Stage II, whereas musical intelligence may be at Stage I or for some at Stage IV.

Developmental psychologists claim emotional development is essential for mature brain development. It may be that as growth occurs, some lines become more mutually interdependent in order to advance, for example, intelligences that nurture a greater capacity to work interdependently. Evidence suggests that Stage IIB and Stage IIIA are where emotional and moral developments become a priority focus, to the extent that one will not progress to Stage IV without both emotional and moral value integration; thus, the focus on ethics and moral authority, and the affirmed assumption that Servant-leadership is necessarily moral leadership. An implication of coming to understand and use the human development models is that it allows us to foresee that the pursuit of wholeness may involve greater integrations of some, and possibly more combinations, of the lines of intelligences.

2nd Tier Integration

Integration is a major theme for Servant-leaders in training. If we assume that all fundamental change, whether personal or organizational, occurs at the spiritual level first, then the human spirit is involved in all human and organizational development. Integration involves continuously reorienting all aspects of our interior and exterior development, and this involves spiritual work. The integration process draws immeasurably on creative imagination, spirit, and our historical experience. Development may be in part ignited by the experience of increasing complexity and fragmentation and a yearning within the human spirit for a greater sense of wholeness for oneself and for the collective.

Greenleaf described *entheos* as the inspiration to serve-first. Entheos inspires profound gratitude, joy, compassion, and generosity and calls forth a servant-consciousness. To become aware of entheos requires the awareness to search for it. For Servant-leaders in training, we will be reminded of entheos as we pass the signposts on our journey toward Servant-leadership. For example, we may be able to recognize the evidence of entheos when we realize, through reflection, that we have shifted (to some extent) from a Stage II worldview to a Stage III worldview, and we identify the seemingly new creative energy that has released within us, and its effect on ourselves and those close to us.

An expansion of consciousness is a result of actuated entheos. A Stage III worldview does not ignore the realities of earlier views and practices of the business world, but rather incorporates them into a broader, more ethical, more inclusive and expansive perspective, and thus a person may address the same issues, policies, or competitive threats and, as a result of entheos, view all that is to be considered from a more expansive perspective. Entheos is what gives us the inspiration, vitality, initiative, and creative energy to do that. When we are prepared to accept what is to come, and what is to go, we receive an abundance of creative energy to step out into the unknown—come what may.

Entheos eventually awakens the call to take responsibility for the world, moving us into action and relationship with all people and to promote human dignity in all its aspects. We engage in the preservation of nature and protection of ecosystems. This is the basis for an ethics of love. The experience of love enables us to overcome greed, fear, and egocentricity. Only love can open a deeper level of consciousness which culminates in universal love; this inspired awareness is a means to healing our fragmented world (Jager, 2010, p. 25). Spiritual integration ignites the values integrations that occur in Stage III and Stage IV development.

Stage III Integrations

Organizationally, integration engages systems thinking, redesigning, reframing, and generative thinking. Hall (1994) identifies four key areas that require integrations necessary to move through IIB–IIIA: knowledge integration, intimacy integration, team integration, and peer integration. The four integrations are critical to Stage III development and serve as the foundation work for Stage IIIB where the *independence–interdependence* dynamic becomes a grounding priority for a serving-first value system and a servant-consciousness.

Knowledge Integration

Our knowledge is formed, informed, and transformed through our creative (imaginal) capacity. Knowledge integration involves, for example, learning a comprehensive philosophy of leadership, or a new system, or a new expanded more integrated worldview. Knowledge integration occurs through study, reflection, intuition, and insight tested in the crucible of experience and reason. For leadership, study of some kind is essential to enhance the integration of instrumental, relational, imaginal, and system skills. Important to this creative integrative process is the nurture of the serving-first disposition. This nurturing is a conscious discipline of daily, hourly, moment-to-moment practices, such as asking, how can I serve this person, this situation, this community? Practice calls forth greater humility over the long term.

Knowledge integration is about enhancing clarity. In a sense it is about learning a greater more coherent worldview—or perceived truth. The most remarkable thing about truth is that when we glimpse it, hear it, see it, feel it, understand it, we know it is so, there is something right about it, it can no longer be denied, and other knowledge comes into clearer focus. We know with greater clarity, in some instances, our way of being in the world may be radically changed as a result; we cannot go back to a lesser awareness. When we speak our truth (as we understand it), it often calls forth the truth from others. Integrating knowledge is about putting what we know into a more expansive, more inclusive perspective, and this involves practicing conceptualization.

Conceptualization engages the articulation of insights, ideas, theories, and the interpretation of reality as we see it. One aspect of conceptualizing is a clarification process focused on developing precise logical reasoning. Another aspect involves describing the bigger picture—knitting things together so to speak. Conceptualizing also involves, while drawing on those aspects already mentioned, projecting our ideas into the future using creative insight and capacity of pathfinding-foresight. Conceptualizing uses skills learned from much practice at reflection on our personal, and organizational, experience and knowing. The ongoing practice of integrating and articulating our intuitions, experience, ideas, and vision exercises the imaginal skills, and our systems' thinking skills become more refined. One can practice conceptualization by paying attention to one's insights and articulating them by way of journaling, and formal written and oral articulation. Conceptualization enhances our knowledge integration.

Intimacy Integration

The capacity for intimacy arises from our relational capacity. Servant-leaders in training develop relational values and skills, learning how to lead in ways that respectfully nurture, retain, and enhance relationships. Leaders need a sound support system at home, at work, and outside of work as they are continuously having their values and skills put to the test. Having one's values supported by even a few intimate friends is affirming. We need others with whom we can express and test our knowledge clarity. Examples include the intimacy that develops between a mentor and mentee, or a coach and players, or between business partners; there can even be a level of intimacy between competitive rivals. What is important is that intimacy occurs within a professional moral context. Work related relational intimacy is about respectfully calling forth and being called forth. When we are accepted for who we are and what we can contribute, we experience a sense of internal self-worth and fulfillment.

There are few things more healing than a healthy life giving relationship. Servant-leaders in training need long-term trusting relationships with people with whom they can discuss the most meaningful things—

including fear, anger, pain, guilt, and shame—and with whom they can laugh, affirm, and celebrate the tender joys of life. Intimate relationships are integral for developing emotional and moral intelligence (EQ and MQ). Enhancing our capacity for intimacy involves a regular ongoing interaction with friends, a spiritual director, elder, sponsor, mentor, companion; the role is not as important as the mutual commitment to journey together along the Servant-leader path. A benefit of relational intimacy is learning to balance and value personal and work relationships.

Team Integration

Team integration involves calling forth people and promoting community. Promoting community involves creating environments where individuals and the collective both flourish—one should not occur at the expense of the other. To put this into practice, we need to identify the values that enhance group flourishing and work at integrating them into our way of being and into our organizational systems. Promoting community is about creating a sense of belonging, alleviating our deep sense of separateness, and that of others. It is about healing and nurturing our capacity for intersubjectivity; this includes awareness, healing, and calling forth our family, community, and societal culture. Team integration is a meso individual and collective actualization where all members may practice an *independent–interdependent* dynamic while being committed to something greater than themselves. Accountability flows out of the connectedness of the community to the whole, and the quality of accountability flows from our willingness to engage through listening-first, valuing questions, and valuing feedback. Thinking of our organization as a community is helpful as our perceived collective identity influences the quality of our accountability and credibility.

Team integration ensures that in a crisis leadership can be delegated. Organizations need leaders able to work within collaborative structures so each group can function at its known values level. Team integrations nurture valuing what Greenleaf called *first among equals* leadership. Designated leaders within each group need to be able to conceptualize and actualize the values that reflect the corporate structures while collaborating and networking with other groups in the system to coordinate system functioning.

Peer Integration

Viewing others as peers requires humility. Outmost respect requires a profoundly humble love for our self, and that love is then naturally related to the desire to serve, and it extends through our worldview. When we treat ourselves with dignity, we can expect and accept it from others, and if we expect to be treated with dignity by others, then they deserve to be treated with dignity also—even when they do not appear or act worthy of it. When we are not being respectful of others, we are being disrespectful to ourselves. When others are not being respectful of us, we draw on our integrity and act with compassion. Listening-first, to self and other(s) with discerning empathy, awareness, and compassion, is an integrating process.

Peer integration involves embracing diversity, humility, respect, acceptance, and tolerance. Integrated organizational policies and systems invite peer group consultation. A professional peer network provides the leader with personal support and reinforces the awareness that leadership is in fact a plural and collaborative venture. As we work to embrace these four integrations, we humbly and slowly learn that everyone is a peer in some way—nurturing a *there I am also* awareness.

Stage IV Integrations

Humanity seems to have been developing Stage II since the last great Renaissance (1300–1700). Is it going to take another 500 years to fully develop Stage III? We live in an age of information acceleration. Humanity appears to be in a major shift toward relational-related values and skills. Our systems and organizations are in the same developmental process; but in many cases, the systems and organizations seem stuck. What do we do when we are stuck? We dig deep and get creative.

As we move toward Stage IV awareness and integration, we move toward greater harmony and systems integration. Where the integrations involved for Stage III development are primarily centered on expanding our personal *independent–interdependent* relational capacities, the integrations called for at Stage IV call for greater focus on the collective *independent–interdependent* capacities. Transitioning to Stage IV involves the most integrative work of our lives.

When our spiritual energy is integrated, our motives and expectations change, so that distrust, animosity, and fear diminish somewhat as they can be held in a non-reactive state. Stage IV development is about accepting responsibility for transforming social, political, and economic realities. Our awareness of being part of the whole places upon us an obligation to contribute to and serve the greater good. Integration at Stage IV involves renewing, valuing, holding, and articulating ancient wisdom and, where and when appropriate, integrating knowledge and information with wisdom as we search for a global clarity to guide human flourishing.

Figure 3.1 shows that most of us are still in the process of completing Stage III, while some of us are venturing into Stage IV. Tier Two is not completed because we, as a leadership group, are just now moving into serious engagement with serving-first, and the challenge of integrating individual and collective actualization in such a way that both the individual and the collectives flourish together. All of which is a holistic endeavor and which will take a tremendous individual and collective creative effort.

Disharmony in our systems is evidence of the need for Stage IV integrations. The ecological divide, the sociological divide, and the spiritual–cultural divides are examples of disruptions in our global harmony (Scharmer & Kaufer, 2013). The three divides are keeping human endeavors fragmented at the micro, meso, macro, and global levels, harming ourselves, all of humanity, and the earth itself. The ecological divide is based on a human disconnect between self and nature, the social divide is a disconnection between self and other (relational), and the spiritual–cultural divide reflects a disconnect between self and Self (p. 4). Scharmer indicates that these divides come into our awareness as personal or collective disruptions. These disruptions provide clear evidence that our created organizational systems are out of harmony. In our time, there seems to be more and more disruptions in our global organizational systems and societies.

Interestingly, when we strive to move toward greater harmony, we quickly become aware of and experience the disharmony more abruptly, as disruptions; we feel it in our bodies, hearts, and minds, and we more clearly perceive it in our culture and organizational systems (Wilber, 2006). Stage IV is about moving toward greater harmony while embracing and nurturing greater diversity. The greater the diversity within a human system, the greater its capacity for healing, creative learning, and resiliency. For Servant-leaders in training the work of Stage IV is about integrating the interior with the exterior. It is about learning a new notion of wholeness by going beyond the rational and learning to access transrational wisdom.

The shift from Stage III to Stage IV calls forth a great surge in our creative capacities as we strive to create a more inclusive and expansive integrated worldview. The interdependent *WE* responds to the common call to work for global harmony, to care for and renew the earth (Generative-servant). Individuals experience themselves humbly functioning as a "WE" (with others) to enhance the quality of life: I–You: We/It. The dawning of a global consciousness is seen as a series of responsibilities to be undertaken with other like-minded people to care for the world.

As with the notion of an independence–interdependence dynamic, the pluses of competition and collaboration give rise to the notion of a synergistic competitive–collaborative dynamic. At Stage IV the notion of competition is finally balanced and integrated with synergistic collaboration. A common hangover from our earlier Stage I and II value systems is our perspective on competition and collaboration. Competition retains a high status and is deemed somewhat sacred in our society. Much of economics and commerce is anchored in our culturally embedded notions of competition. Competition is instinctual to human nature. Looking out for "number one" hones our skills and teaches us to strive, compete, and adapt. Individually, as teams, corporately, and as nations we have become very good at competitive, defensive, and offensive techniques and strategy. Somewhat similarly, collaborative competition makes us strong as a team, a group, a nation. Competition is inherent in our individual and organizational development, and a cornerstone of an I–You, us against them, value system. Be that as it is, greater competition was not what Greenleaf was calling for; he was calling for greater relational and systems collaboration.

Ethical competition fosters foundational values for highly functional collaboration. The values and skills involved with collaboration are more relationally complex and expansively inclusive than those involved with competition. Collaboration calls for a relational dynamic that assumes congruent autonomy and harmonious mutual benefits (independence–interdependence) within a dynamic open system. I suspect that when humanity becomes as experienced, skilled, and adept at synergistic collaboration as we now are at competing, we will have progressed significantly, and competition will not be as singularly sacred as it is currently extolled to be. This does not mean that we will no longer use competition developmentally, but we will also have more highly refined collaborative skill and value capacities that embrace an *all of us together* value system.

Synergistic collaboration involves stimulating collective intelligence. Today our organizations are becoming increasingly complex, so complex that we need to awaken our capacity for collective intelligence to resolve the system challenges needed to revitalize our organizations and communities. We need to collectively envision and design the system changes by drawing on individual and collective intelligence. How can we learn to call forth collective intelligence? This question is asked from the *WE* perspective; it is a Servant-leader question. A challenge for Servant-leaders in training is learning how to nurture collective intelligence (collective wisdom) in a reliable way. Stage IV is about becoming adept at a more advanced stage of calling forth and using collective intelligence.

References

Beck, D. E., & Cowan, C. C. (2006). *Spiral dynamics: Mastering values, leadership, and change.* Malden, MA: Blackwell.
Bloom, A. (Ed.). (Trans.)(1968). *The republic of Plato.* New York: Basic Books.
Delman, R. (2018). *Personal communication.* Sebatopol, CA: The Embodied Life School.

Feldenkrais, M. (1977). *Awareness through movement: Easy-to-do health exercises to improve your posture, vision, imagination, and personal awareness.* San Francisco: Harper Collins.

Greenleaf, R. K. (1977). *Servant leadership: A journey into the nature of legitimate power and greatness.* New York: Paulist Press.

Hall, B. P. (1994). *Values shift: A guide to personal & organizational transformation.* Rockport, MA: Twin Lights.

Jager, W. (2010). *Eternal timeless wisdom: The wisdom underlying all spiritual paths* (M.-A. H. Horstemke, Trans.). Kosel-Vaerlag.

Jaworski, J. (2012). *Source: The inner path of knowledge creation.* San Francisco: Barrett-Koehler.

Scharmer, O., & Kaufer, K. (2013). *Leading from the emerging future: From ego-system to eco-system economies.* San Francisco: Barrett-Koehler.

Wilber, K. (2006). *Integral spirituality: A startling new role for religion in the modern world.* Boston, MA: Integral Books.

Zohar, D., & Marshall, I. (2004). *Spiritual capital: Wealth we can live by.* San Francisco: Barrett-Koehler.

4

Empathetic and Moral

Profoundly Relational

Greenleaf (1972) proposed that Servant-leadership is "a practical philosophy which supports people who choose to serve-first, and then lead as a way of expanding service to individuals and society" (p. 1). To comprehend what Greenleaf meant, we need to experience a creative re-conceptualization of our notion of leadership: we need new insights. Greenleaf understood this. He deliberately fused the concepts servant and leader with a hyphen *Servant-leader* because he wanted to create a new conceptualization of leadership—a concept that initiates a disruption in our thinking. Adding servant as a modifier to the traditional notions of leading creates a conceptual struggle that needs a metamorphosis to constellate and contextualize a profoundly relational leading disposition.

Currently our society is in the process of transforming our traditional concept of service into a more complex and comprehensive understanding. In a sense we are conceptualizing a value-laden new meaning in our understanding and our working language. To help our conceptualizing, imagine a progression in your understanding that flows from *slave to servant—servant to steward—steward to Servant-leader.* Conceptually our

© The Author(s) 2018
J. H. Horsman, *Servant-Leaders in Training,*
Palgrave Studies in Workplace Spirituality and Fulfillment,
https://doi.org/10.1007/978-3-319-92961-3_4

awareness seems to experience an expansion of freedom, purpose, and responsibility as our definitional understanding flows to each more informed perspective. For example, the traditional notion of stewardship is associated with competent, responsible management: that notion of stewardship is now expanding to include the philosophical assumptions of Servant-leadership. Stewardship within Servant-leadership entails a more comprehensive (global) responsibility than just competent, efficient, legal oversight. The expanded other-oriented perspective of servant-stewardship assumes the responsibility to develop others, combined with a congruence in what we say, how we relate, and what we model. Related to this is Greenleaf's notion of *first among equals* and the assumption that Servant-leadership is plural, ensuring that leadership progression should never become a crisis. The expanding responsibility of stewardship also includes a moral authority that seeks a specific and general good in light of Greenleaf's test. The stewardship of the wise caring elder looks to the general good of the whole as well as the specific while applying systems thinking and strategies essential to the long-term as well as the short-term micro, meso, macro, mundo vision.

Similar to the transitioning of meaning from stewardship to Servant-leadership, there are somewhat parallel changes occurring with our notion of followership. In recent years, authors have been redefining followership (i.e., Kellerman, 2008); the term is also experiencing a metamorphosis as it transforms from slave to subordinate toward notions of supportive, participative, collaborative, and even peer leader. These fundamental changes in our conceptualization of stewardship and followership provide evidence and support for our evolving and more expansive conceptualization of Servant-leadership.

Greenleaf's (1977) notion of *serving-first* qualifies and contextualizes the relational purpose for leading. What is most interesting about Greenleaf's explanation is that the context for leading comes prior to the hyphen; the great difference in Servant-leadership is that wanting to serve signifies a value-laden socio-centricity that arises as a relational feeling rather than an objective idea. The distinction reveals the root of the conceptual struggle with Greenleaf's philosophy, we have to first identify with the feeling, and the experience, of wanting to serve-first, before we can really know it and rationally conceptualize it; this means that true comprehension of this concept involves some heart–mind integration. It seems we need to engage our emotional intelligence (EQ) and our moral intelligence (MQ) to fuse the concept with our cognitive understanding before we can make sense of this complex leadership philosophy.

Another significant insight arising from Greenleaf's statements is that the choice to *serve-first* is radically different from choosing to lead for power, or recognition. In developmental theory, the desire for power and recognition arises foremost within the struggle from dependence toward independence, whereas the natural desire to serve-first arises foremost within the transition from dependence toward interdependence. Servant-leadership is a form of leadership that emerges developmentally from a more expansive integrated view of the world. Accordingly, Servant-leadership carries vital energies, values, and wisdom at a transformative depth that many may not yet be aware of.

Moral Authority

If what we do is unethical, it is not Servant-leadership. Coming to understand *moral authority* is another insightful way to grasp Servant-leadership because it represents a reciprocal inter-reliance between leader and follower, as opposed to just the moral view of a leader. Moral authority is mutually developed and shared between people and engages a mutual relational commitment to the creation of human flourishing. Moral authority is sustained by an interdependent purpose grounded in accepted universal human values and a mutually shared vision. As such, Servant-leaders model a principle-centered empathetic moral capacity.

"We come into the world to be interdependent; furthermore, if we do not work to serve others, we fail to act as morally intelligent leaders" (Lennick & Kiel, 2005, p. 100). Moral intelligence is a recognized human capacity (Wilber's *lines of intelligence*). Moral intelligence (MQ) shows we have the cognitive capacity to regulate how human principles should be applied through the discernment of meaning, values, and purpose and through our judgments and actions (Lennick & Kiel, 2005). Moral intelligence enhances our capacity for listening, reflecting on, and discerning the moral consequences of our reasoning, judgment, decisions, and actions. Moral intelligence stimulates a mutual relational commitment for the creation of human flourishing. Such a relational commitment can be examined with the application of Greenleaf's *test* of Servant-leadership.

> *The best test, and the most difficult to administer is: Do those served grow as persons? Do they, while being served, become healthier, wiser, freer, more autonomous, more likely themselves to become servants? And what is the effect on the least privileged in society; will they benefit or, at least, not be further deprived?* (Greenleaf, 1977, pp. 13–14)

Greenleaf knew the application of the benchmark *test* would always be difficult to apply; nevertheless, he claimed it is the best test for Servant-leadership. For Servant-leaders in training, moral authority summons caring, compassion, and generosity, all of which assume interdependence and profound respect toward self and others. The moral-relational focus of Servant-leadership ensures that the focus is on serving others for the purpose of creating responsible individuals, groups, and organizations and a more caring productive society.

Empathy and Compassion

Moral ethical issues generally become more clarified in our value system during Stage IIB and Stage III development; however, research indicates that the foundations of moral intelligence are with us from birth and emerge from an innate capacity for empathy. We all are in a sense hard-wired for morality. Empathy is a crucial building block of moral intelligence and is foundational for our human morality. Empathy, however, needs to be nurtured and modeled (called forth) for one's moral development to progress. A critical aspect of this progress is learning to become authentically empathetic with ourselves. Essentially, this involves a capacity for healing and forgiving ourselves, others, and moving on.

Nurturing empathy often involves enhancing our inner awareness and doing healing work. The benefit of doing personal healing work is that we become more available to engage in healthy relationships and are able to become authentically empathetic when the emotions of others resonate with similar or identifiable emotions within ourselves. Empathy involves learning to listen and that involves humility, and a capacity to be present and available even in the midst of apparent chaos or rejection. Empathy is "reflecting and experiencing other people's feelings and states of being through a quality of presence that has the consequence of their seeing themselves with more clarity, even without any words being spoken" (Hall, 1994, p. 228).

Speculatively, empathy may be an essential aspect of the experience of love and may be operationally present within the desire to serve-first. The relational choice to serve-first seems intricately associated with mutual empathy. Empathy respectfully leans toward embracing a *there I am also* perspective, and it engages and potentially evolves relationships. A *there I am also* perspective is more inclusive and empathetic than *me, myself, and I*, or *you and me against the world*, or *us versus them* perspectives. As we transcend from dependence to independence, toward *independence–interdependence*, our focus transforms from valuing *I–You* to increasingly valuing an *I–You* perspective. Respectfully valuing others as a *You*, with a capital Y, in part implies increasing respectful empathy for others.

As empathy is a cornerstone of moral development, it is involved in making moral ethical decision and taking moral ethical actions. A holistic integration of empathy (heart and mind) is foundational to developing a capacity for moral logic. When Servant-leaders apply Greenleaf's *test*, they are using moral logic. Moral logic involves listening, and discerning skills, and initiating movement toward greater harmony and holism, and a more caring society.

An empathetic relational perspective obliges Servant-leaders in training to work to create morally intelligent organizations. A morally intelligent organization is built on profoundly relational, creative, holistic, and integral values. Morally intelligent organizations have a culture with systems and programs infused with values that promote human flourishing and whose members learn to consistently act in ways that promote alignment with those values.

Compassion is a complex value that arises from empathy, love, and humility and heartens our quest for beauty, goodness, and truth. Compassion like empathy is operationalized internally and externally in how we relate to ourselves and how we relate to others. Compassion presents an option to transcend our more limited perspectives, and in the acceptance and perhaps forgiveness of self and others, we find the compassion that heals. Compassion calls forth the responsibility to serve and care for others. Compassion involves supporting the choices of others, caring as much as they do, and sometimes even caring more about what is good for them—then they do. Compassion at times compels an intrusion into other people's lives; intrusions that are respect-filled and moral and consider both the individual and the collective good.

Compassion also stimulates moral intelligence. Similar to building trust, visible compassionate acts are remembered and convey a yearning to pass it on. Servant-leaders in training strive to build organizations that have a capacity for compassion toward all whom they serve by using compassion when applying and interpreting their systems and policies. A compassionate organization, for example, can be identified by the way it handles layoffs, or by the way senior leaders compassionately receive and respond to criticism. A thumb rule for compassion is: *when in doubt err on the side of generosity.*

Integrity and Responsibility

Empathy for oneself shines an interior light on the notion of integrity. Integrity is central aspect of moral intelligence and integral to moral development. Historically, notions of integrity emerged from Roman military tradition:

> During the time of the 12 Caesars, the Roman army would conduct morning inspections. As the inspecting centurion would come in front of each legionnaire, the soldier would strike with his right fist the armor breastplate that covered his heart. The armor had to be strongest there in order to protect the heart from the sword thrusts and from arrow strikes. As the soldier struck his armor, he would shout "integritas" (in-teg-ri-tas), which in Latin means material, wholeness, completeness, and entirety. The inspecting centurion would listen closely for this affirmation and also for the ring that well-kept armor would give off. Satisfied that the armor was sound and that the soldier beneath it was protected, he would then move on to the next man. (Krulak, 2000)

The essence of this meaning of integrity still holds in that what is visible on the outside must be entirely consistent with the interior disposition. What we know about integrity however is that it gets tested with every ethical dilemma and personal conflict we experience. Where the centurion searches for integrity from the outside in, exemplifying 1st Tier (Stages I–II) development, at 2nd Tier (Stages III–IV) integrity manifests from the inside out. Integrity is the inner sense of congruence, faith, and knowing; the *I am* that stands firm; without integrity *I wobble*. Integrity is the enactment of one's authenticity and awareness and our preparedness to act morally and responsibly in the world. Our integrity allows us to stand humbly and compassionately firm against temptation, chaos, confusion, misinformation, threats, and personal attack.

Our experience, awareness, and learning teach us that striving to maintain our integrity is an ongoing journey. Personal integrity involves acting consistently with our principles, values, and beliefs, such as telling the truth, standing up for what is right, and keeping promises. Acting with integrity may involve exposing and removing dishonesty, repelling slander, restoring justice and truth, respecting our neighbor, defending our dignity, and that of others, refusing immorality, making the right choice between good options, shunning scams and deceptions, rejecting manipulation and exploitation, and choosing to act on faith. Integrity like trust forms incrementally and similarly erodes at light speed. Integrity calls forth ongoing interior vigilance and is an ongoing endeavor.

How do we nurture and develop integrity? Compassionate awareness of our lapses of integrity is a huge beginning point; additionally, we enhance integrity by practicing certain virtuous practices or disciplines— disciplines such as patience, honesty, humility (there are hundreds of human virtue). By striving to overcome impediments to honesty, for example, we reinforce the discipline and that in turn enhances our integrity. Consciously practicing a discipline requires that we attend to and listen internally to our intentions and inclinations, our instincts, and our automatic behavior responses. Often, the prideful, negative, and justifying tapes we play in our head require some adjustment when examined with self-honesty and Greenleaf's test.

What is relevant for personal integrity is also relevant for organizational leadership. Integrity keeps organizations together. Integrity encourages loyal and trustworthy employees. Responsible organizational leaders embrace service to others and acknowledge service to others by producing worthwhile products or services and creating a socially worthwhile mission. Integrity entails being willing to admit mistakes and failures, taking responsibility for personal choices, embracing responsibility for serving, and calling forth others. When we act responsibly, we reinforce and model integrity.

Greenleaf suggested that we should assume unlimited liability for our choices. Responsibility involves making informed and reasonable judgments, making decisions, and taking action toward greater flourishing. Responsibility is accepting that we are accountable to ourselves as well as others. Responsibility begins with a concern for self, to receive the education and inward growth that provides the serenity of spirit that affirms an interior freedom to morally move in an appropriate direction. With that sense of freedom, we respond to the exterior environment, striving to make a worthwhile contribution, beginning with a concern for members of our family, neighbors, work groups, community, and our global society (Greenleaf, 1977). As we become more aware, our sense of personal and societal responsibility expands. At some point in our awareness and learning (Stage III), we realize that we have an obligation to be reflective, informed, and self-aware, and we can no longer be non-responsible. Accepting responsibility for all that we do may seem overwhelming, but we do it anyway.

Forgiveness and Healing

Forgiveness and healing are closely related aspects of a profoundly relational Servant-leader disposition. Forgiveness, similar to compassion, impacts on how we relate to ourselves and others. Forgiveness involves becoming open to reconciliation and restorative justice. Self-forgiving is accepting we have faults and that we make mistakes. Self-forgiving involves letting go of self-anger for our past failures and misjudgments. It even means letting go of the need to work so hard to make up for our past offenses. Self-forgiveness entails no longer needing penance, sorrow, and regret; it involves nurturing self-healing and self-love that comes with lightening the burden of guilt and shame. Forgiving others involves accepting faults and mistakes of others and allowing and respectfully honoring their own self-forgiveness process and personally choosing to let go and move on.

Forgiving heals relationships; it involves doing what is necessary to restore the relationship, respectfully and prudently. Forgiveness can be the most challenging enactment of love imaginable. When we are hurt, self-protection arises. We tend to withdraw into our shell or automatically strike out projecting venom; neither resolves the issue. In a sense all forgiveness is self-forgiveness, for whenever we close our hearts, become cold hearted, we suffer, and those around us suffer. Becoming warm hearted is more than a cognitive awareness or choice, it involves going to the heart of our being and examining the attitudes and judgments we hold against ourselves, forgiving ourselves for our false assumptions, and sometimes even forgiving our instinctual self. Healing our cold heartedness changes our perspective and that of others toward us, and themselves.

Morally intelligent organizations use forgiveness as a fundamental and innovative growth strategy (Lennick & Kiel, 2005, p. 7). Forgiveness involves having tolerance for mistakes and acknowledging our own imperfections, without which we are likely to be rigid, inflexible, and unable to engage with others in ways that promote a mutual good.

> Socially, both forgiveness and the disciplined process of reconciliation draw us into a crucible from which we can emerge more refined, more willing to see the heart of another, and more able to create just and lasting relationships. Such relationships—robust—durable—enjoyable—courageous— form what is best in people, in families, and in the workplace. The will to seek forgiveness, the will to forgive and the will to pursue reconciliation may be a significant part of developing the kind of wisdom, health, autonomy, and freedom espoused by Robert Greenleaf in his idea of the Servant-leader, and idea whose time has arrived, an idea that is destined to remain.... (Ferch, 2003, p. 1)

A forgiving community creates an environment where people know that failing is part of being human, accepting that we all fail at times stimulates aware healing and creative learning.

Healing is involved with developing integrity, becoming responsible, conveying compassion and forgiveness. Healing is often essential for learning. When we learn to *pause* between the stimulus and our automatic response, our boundaries, biases, and defensive barriers may be breached with new awareness and clearer understanding. In this context, healing is about being present and available enough to let go of the old (behavior patterns and belief systems) and become open to what may come, or what is emerging. Healing often occurs when we are accepting, open, and humble. Aware healing and creative learning are two interrelated ways to grow as adults, *learn-heal–heal-learn*, and are integral to the motivation for serving and greater wholeness.

We need others if we are to become fully human. Healing for many adults forges humility and a greater depth of learning. As human beings we are created for relationships ultimately for love expressed through the appreciation and realization of the beauty, goodness, and truth among us. Becoming more relationally responsible is an endeavor for Servant-leaders in training.

Servant-Leaders Promote Community

A basic test of a philosophy is its universality. Greenleaf prescribed Servant-leadership for all. Servant-leaders function within all stages of human development and in many kinds of organizations. The inference is that most organizations, regardless of the type, culture, or location, may benefit from Servant-leadership.

> Our interconnectedness with other people moves us to greater service, to a more profound understanding, appreciation, and tolerance of one another; to an honest self-examination of our own attitudes, and behavior; and to the building of community. (Beazley, 2003, p. 5)

Often when we begin to study Servant-leadership, we do not initially see its universality; however, when we begin to reflect on the Servant-leader(s) in our lives and share that experience with others, we find that there are Servant-leaders in all kinds of roles and occupations.

Servant-leading is much more than a style of leadership, it is an attitudinal disposition, a way of being, a worldview that integrates and uses a variety of styles of leadership that are appropriate to a particular situation or environment. For example, a Servant-leader may be autocratic at times, because that is the most appropriate way of dealing with an issue or situation; however, that response is rooted in an emerging servant-consciousness. A servant disposition is not something that can be chosen one moment and then put away the next (at least not for long). Servant-leading, in its fullness, reflects a way of being and a value-based relational framework for interpreting, reasoning, judging, deciding, and acting. Serving-first contextualizes a relational priority and the purpose for leadership, and all else that one does. As a worldview, Servant-leaders include all humanity and the living and material world a stewardship responsibility, a mystery in which we must participate and for which we must responsibly care. Servant-leadership is a universal philosophy for leadership; its purpose is to nurture human wholeness and human flourishing.

Servant-leaders in training acknowledge that the people they work with are vital to the flourishing of their organizations. They strive to maintain, nurture, and generally promote community through their commitment to serving-first and their awareness of the interconnectedness of all people. Servant-leaders endeavor to directly or indirectly promote a sense of belonging and encourage others to become involved in projects that challenge them to support and participate in the good of the collective. Promoting community involves practicing relational values that call for a more integrated holistic global systems framework for working with collective systems.

At Stages III and IV of human development, Servant-leaders promote community through nurturing and reexamining the human yearning for enhanced identity, meaning, and purpose. Such endeavors involve engaging the individual's sense of worth by providing opportunities to serve and by engaging their yearning for a deeper, richer, more authentic community experience. We all yearn for more authentic fulfilling community experience. Authentic community is created on trust and integrity, where respectful acceptance, a sense of worth, and belonging are foundational, where individuals can speak their truths in an environment of empathetic and generative listening, and where they can actively engage in generative meaningful and creative dialog.

Independence–Interdependence

The Jesuit philosopher, Bernard Lonergan, proposed that human development is nurtured in community. Human flourishing

> is at once individual and social. Individuals do not just operate to meet their needs but cooperate to meet one another's needs. As the community develops its institutions to facilitate cooperation, so individuals develop skills to fulfill the roles and perform the tasks set by the institutional framework. Though the roles are fulfilled and the tasks are performed that the needs be met, still all is done not blindly but knowingly, not necessarily but freely. The progress is not merely the service of man; it is above all the making of man, his advancement in authenticity, the fulfillment of his affectivity, and the direction of his work to the particular goods and a good of order that are worthwhile. (Lonergan in Morelli & Morelli, 2002, p. 464)

Most human development models place the primary focus on tracking the development of the individual, with a more limited importance placed on the role of community engagement. Maslow's well-known *Hierarchy of Needs* is an example (see Table 2.1, Chap. 2). Although Maslow clearly emphasized the importance of community, overtime, his model has increasingly become perceived as the individual's quest for self-actualization, as if self-actualization occurs naturally irrespective of collective engagement. The issue is not that community collectives are being ignored in social research, rather the issue is that self-actualization and community actualization are not being associated as two aspects of an *independence–interdependence* dynamic.

The (disproportionate) diagram in Fig. 4.1 is derived from Chap. 1, Fig. 1.1, and Blackfoot heritage. The larger light spiral represents the cumulative collective historical development of culture, organizations, community collectives, and systems (lower half of Wilber's four quadrants, tipped 90 degrees to the left). The dark spiral represents individual development (upper half of Wilber's four quadrants, tipped 90 degrees to the right). The greater one's individual development, the greater the potential influence of a contribution to collective perpetuity. Also, the greater the accumulated development of many individuals, the greater the contribution of the potential for influencing

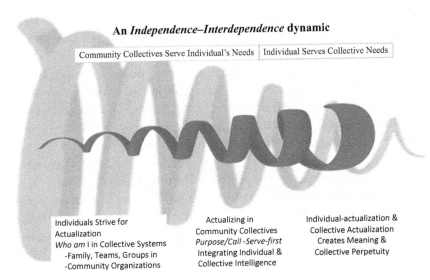

An *Independence–Interdependence* dynamic

| Community Collectives Serve Individual's Needs | Individual Serves Collective Needs |

Individuals Strive for
Actualization
Who am I in Collective Systems
 -Family, Teams, Groups in
 -Community Organizations

Actualizing in
Community Collectives
Purpose/Call -Serve-first
Integrating Individual &
Collective Intelligence

Individual-actualization &
Collective Actualization
Creates Meaning &
Collective Perpetuity

Fig. 4.1 Individual and collective actualization. Printed with permission of Gonzaga University

collective perpetuity. Community actualization occurs from individuals acting independently and interdependently. As individuals move toward self-actualization, their community involvement bears greater fruit supporting and creating collective actualization and collective perpetuity.

Michel (2014) claimed that Maslow's model was influenced by Blackfoot philosophy, emphasizing that self-actualization is foundational to collective actualization and that the most valued contribution a person can make promotes *cultural perpetuity* (ongoing collective flourishing). An interpretive adaptation of Maslow's drive for self-actualization and Blackstock's narrative shown in Fig. 4.1 blends individual development with a depiction of Bloodstock's notion of the individual's service to the collective cultural heritage. The individual human quest for self-actualization ultimately pursued through experiences and understanding of beauty, goodness, and truth, along with the collective manifestation of *collective perpetuity* expressed through ultimate meaning understood by multiple individuals, within multiple groups, organizations, and communities striving to respond to and understand the philosophical human questions: who am I; what is my purpose; what is most meaningful in our ongoing pursuit of evolving and enduring wisdom.

Figure 4.1 reveals some important insights. First, that notions of self-actualization can be harmonized with the need for collective actualization. Figure 4.1 supports Greenleaf's statement that wanting to serve is a *natural* feeling, a feeling that naturally desires collective actualization, because in promoting collective actualization self-actualization and greater wholeness may be realized. The individual and the collectives are not only interdependent but dynamically synergistic; they function together to enhance each other, actualizing collectives support self-actualization and vice versa, and the more they enhance each other, the greater the individual and collective flourishing. The difference is that the collective does not have a single independent mind, but rather a complex collective yearning to influence the independence of many, albeit in many different ways. In human developmental, Stage III and IV Servant-leaders and Generative-servants (wise elders) serve the collective yearning through the *independence–interdependence* dynamic with a focus on what is most meaningful in light of *collective perpetuity* at the micro, meso, macro, and mundo levels. Servant-leaders and especially Generative-servants assume responsibility for *collective perpetuity* and that is why the role of the wise elder is so important in every era.

The collective does not exist without individuals; if individuals do not contribute to developing *collective perpetuity*, individual, cultural, and systems wisdom will not get passed on and society (similar to an individual) may remain in its current stage, or worse regress to an earlier stage of development (a dark age). Conversely, perhaps the greatest risks of a shift to a new worldview (a new renaissance) are the cultural resistance that arises with the apparent loss of cultural values that accompanies the integration stage of more complex values into a grander worldview. This transition is the very reason we are in need of many wise elders in our era. Wise elders seek the clarity to rearticulate the value priorities, in ways, and in a language that is clear to all regardless of their stage of development. Wise elders are needed to ensure *cultural perpetuity*. (See Chap. 7: "Waking Up the Wise Elder.")

Individuals, groups, organizations, communities, and society hold the cultural values and wisdom that ensure ongoing collective continuity and flourishing—this is the role of our education systems and numerous other organizations that serve to facilitate and promote cultural values.

Collectives are where individuals develop, practice, and evolve their values through the development of their instrumental, relational, system, and imaginal skills in their quest for actualization. The greater the stage of the culture, the greater the cultural flourishing of the collective, and the greater the potential for individual advancement through the stages of development. Unfortunately, there is as equally as great a potential for individuals to negatively influence the collective. The future values of the Stages III and IV that we are evolving toward such as compassion, holism, harmony, and global systems continually call forth the refinement of our current values and their corresponding skills.

The *independence–interdependence* dynamic is a more complex version of the old saying *all for one and one for all* and is motivated by the knowing that serving-first is more fulfilling than self-serving, and grounded with the best test. The dynamic is derived from the assumption that each stage of developmental has an A and a B phase, wherein A is a focus on self-functioning and the B phase focuses on functioning relationally in the collective. The *independence–interdependence* dynamic arises out of Stage II and grows stronger with the realization of the *I–You/We/It* notion and a commitment to serving-first, where at some point the oscillation from self-responsibility (independence) to collective-responsibility (interdependence) becomes an integrated dynamic (in Stage IIIB and through Stage IV development).

The *independence–interdependence* dynamic evolves from shifting values and awareness from self-centric and ethno-centric perspectives toward more expansive and inclusive global-centric and eventually cosmic-centric perspectives. The developmental transition begins with yearning to be free of dependence; the yearning provides energy for movement toward responsible and healthy independence. The yearning to individuate and act out of our authenticity is a natural and basic human drive—a drive that moves us toward autonomous, self-initiating, self-responsible, self-reflective, and self-aware abilities that support the capacity for field independence. Importantly, the *independence–interdependence* dynamic does not diminish our sense of self, but rather enriches our sense of self through serving the interests of the greater good of the collective. Again, promoting healthy interdependence does not mean foregoing our independence; healthy independence actually enhances our capacity for interdependence, and healthy interdependence actually enhances our capacity for independence—a reciprocal dynamic, like breathing in and breathing out each in its purpose affirms, supports, and facilitates the other, for the well-being of the whole system.

Dependence on others is normal; we are all dependent on others to some extent; however, it seems many people get stuck in cognitive or emotional dependence. A particularly difficult personal aspect of the transition from dependence to independence seems to involve getting beyond our need for approval and avoidance of disapproval—I am not sure many of us ever get completely free of these needs. Nevertheless, this natural need for acceptance and approval is essential for developing the sense of self-worth that nurtures independence, providing we don't become stuck in dysfunctional behavioral patterns. Developmentally it takes a lot of personal and relational work to mature beyond the need for acceptance and approval, where we can stand in field independence with our own integrity, creativity, and values, against the storm—or perhaps worse—too much success.

A healthy sense of responsible independence is necessary for healthy interdependence. Independence is necessary to prepare us for working interdependently in healthy (non-codependent) ways. Learning healthy interdependent collaboration entails the integration of complex relational and collegial skills and values that require continuous acknowledgment, practice, and support. Values and related skills associated with interdependence include those that enhance supporting, participating, collaborating, networking, and valuing inclusivity and diversity. A positive personal acknowledgment of the value of interdependence is one of the most significant ingredients to successful collaboration.

A great example of *independence–interdependence* can be drawn from the life of Gandhi. During the campaign for Indian independence, Gandhi once organized a national march from one side of India to the other. Tens of thousands walked with him. Midway through, he suddenly stopped and announced, "No, No, this is a mistake! Turn back!" Appalled, his followers questioned his judgment and consistency. Gandhi replied, "My commitment is not to consistency. My commitment is to do what I think is right at every moment, even if it means saying that I was wrong" (Zohar & Marshall, 2004, p. 96). Zohar describes this kind of independence as field independence (p. 80). To learn to lead with field independence, Servant-leader in training needs to be aware of their responsibility to the collective, regardless of personal consequences. If we do not, we may remain stuck in dysfunctional approval patterns—at great harm to our integrity and the credibility of the collective.

We all experience a continuous back and forth oscillating pull of personal interests and collective interests. The collective process is encouraged through team, group, education, and organizational work. The urge for independence provides a perpetual tension with the collective pull; this tension actually helps pull individuals to a greater stage of actualization and at times holds individuals back from progressing when cultural inflexibly holds on to (does not integrate) an earlier value system such as centralized control or ethno-centricity. Servant-leaders strive to lead the collective from a profoundly relational, creative, holistic, and integrative disposition oscillating from the desire for autonomous (independent) actions to the desire for acting interdependently with the collective. Developing a servant-consciousness, in part, involves the interplay between independence and interdependence becoming an actualized dynamic, such that the focus of attention transitions back and forth from the individual to the collective, from a need for independent thought and action to enhancing collective thought and action. The dynamic is a capacity to act autonomously and interdependently for the good of the collective. Interdependence is about acknowledging and accepting our dependence on others and consciously embracing and working with that reality. We act interdependently when we faithfully accept that collaboration is the most fruitful way to ensure *cultural perpetuity*; we also assume responsibility to act independently to voice and show concern when cultural systems are not facilitating human flourishing.

Congruence and Harmony

When we engage the values, capacities, and dispositions of Servant-leading, we often are put to the test and our incongruities arise before us. Congruence is "the capacity to experience and express one's feelings and thoughts in such a way that what one experiences internally and communicates externally to others are the same" (Hall, 1994, p. 227). Our incongruities become especially evident to us and others during the transition between Stage II and Stage III; if we are not willing to identify and resolve our contradictions in this transition, we will remain stuck between two incongruent worldviews. A significant portion of our Western populations seems to be between these two worldviews, thus the call for Servant-leaders. Congruence and incongruence show up in what we say, how we relate, and perhaps most importantly how we model our values.

Striving for congruence and harmony are natural movements within Stages III and IV. The movement toward congruity at Stage III reflects a natural search for clarity of purpose; this search for clarity involves identifying the contradictions of our beliefs and values in our behaviors and in our organizational systems. Our values become clear and visible to others when we model congruent behavior in our personal life and in our work, and they are reinforced when those values are embedded in our systems. When leader's articulate serving-first values but retain organizational systems that continue to reward self-serving values, followers become disheartened and confused, and distrust arises.

Striving to speak, relate, and congruently model a consistent value system is a Servant-leader responsibility. At the organizational level the chosen organizational values need to be clear and consistently modeled and evident in the vision, mission, strategy, policies, procedures, programs, and systems. As leaders we are models for others and we all know that incongruent thinking, words, and actions create doubt, cynicism, and distrust, whereas congruent actions, relating, and words reveal dependability, inspire confidence, and enhance trust. Figure 4.2 depicts the power of congruent modeling, relating, and influencing at the personal and organizational level.

Servant-leadership, as a way of being, reflects and values personal and organizational congruence and the striving for systems harmony. Harmony is a Stage IV value that further refines our sense of congruence. Congruent harmony is about an integrated balance in the tuning of diverse elements. Congruent harmony can be experienced as a sense of flow within ourselves, or when we achieve system synergies in an organization, or come to understand, appreciate, and celebrate the beauty in

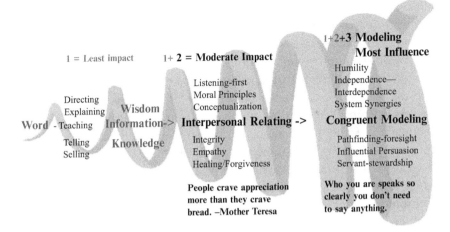

Fig. 4.2 Spiraling influence of congruent word relating and modeling. Congruent words, interpersonal relating, and modeling have the most influential impact on others. Printed with permission of Gonzaga University

the harmony of a diverse ecosystem. Harmony, it seems, has a way of manifesting more magnificence and beauty when diversity and complexity are finely tuned, such that the greater the diversity the greater the harmonic resiliency. Harmony is also associated with humility; when one is humble, one is in harmony with self and others.

Scharmer and Kaufer (2013) offer persuasive evidence that many of our values and created structures are out of harmony with our ecological, sociological, and spiritual–cultural awareness and actions. They advocate for a consciousness shift from *me* to *we*, from ego-systems to eco-systems consciousness. Servant-leaders in training strive to develop a healthy sense of independence so they are able to interdependently use persuasive influence in respectful and progressive ways. When we move toward greater harmony, we begin to experience the disharmony more abruptly; we feel it in our bodies and know it in our minds and, as a result, perceive it with greater clarity. As the world seems to be swirling toward greater fragmentation, we can easily become overwhelmed with the immensity of the global issues. If we do not find a way of viewing these distressing issues from a more expanded inclusive open-hearted perspective, reality can quickly become too overwhelming and painful to bear—leaving us numb and apathetic. Our role is not to deny or minimize reality, but to be more *awake and disturbed* (Greenleaf), to continue to learn and practice perceiving and acting to creatively search for improved systems.

We work to improve our congruity by becoming aware of the incongruities in our contradictory and our counterproductive practices, and with that awareness, we then make adaptive adjustments. We begin with interior listening. Often incongruities arise through listening to silence (meditation). Other practices such as discernment and focusing are helpful. Interior listening leads to better exterior listening. Exteriorly we listen to what we hear ourselves saying, and we listen for the inconsistencies of others to recognize what resides within ourselves; this is humbling work. To promote congruence and harmony at the personal and organizational level, Servant-leaders in training strive to nurture complex values such as compassion, generosity, gratitude, and joy, as complements to empathy, healing, forgiveness, and humility. These are values that are often dismissed, as peripheral to current organizational purpose, efficiency, and success.

Trust

"Nothing will move until trust is firm" (Greenleaf, 1977, p. 101). Servant-leaders know that trust and appropriate relational intimacy foster team synergy and creativity. Promoting trust promotes community and in so doing inspires and calls forth individual and collective creativity. Promoting, calling forth, and modeling interdependent trust are a long-term ongoing undertaking for Servant-leaders. Promoting community is contingent on the test of trust, and congruent modeling nurtures trust.

Trust within a collective seems to increase slowly over time, forming from consistent value-driven purposeful leadership actions and dependable system processes. Gradually an organizational reservoir of trust can be built up; however, trust like most liquids in a reservoir always seems to be seeping and evaporating away, requiring conscious ongoing replenishment. Distrust, on the other hand, evaporates trust at light speed. Breaking trust can be relationally devastating; once lost, distrust can become embedded in relationships and in systems throughout the organization and the community. Similarly to individuals, organizations regress when trust is lost.

The Servant-leader's role, when trust has been lost, is to find some ground where trust exists and begin restoring trust; this may entail returning to the foundational values of a lower stage of development. No matter how fluid, fragmented, or distrustful the environment, there are likely some things in the community or organization that remain constant. Payroll, for example, a Stage I priority, affirms security and needs to be dependable. From a base level of consistent reliable pay, other value constants can be quickly identified and re-affirmed, providing a new foundation for restorative trust.

Trust gets put to the test often, and it is important that Servant-leaders in training pass the test. It is easiest to trust people, or organizations, after they have proven that they are trustworthy. Servant-leaders in training seek ways to call forth the trustworthiness of others. Choosing at times to trust without evidence that trust is warranted and then inviting the other(s) to grow into that trust. Such work takes courage and an act of faith; however, it is a way to call others forth, and it promotes commitment, and loyalty. Building trust promotes community and in so doing inspires and calls forth individual and collective creativity.

References

Beazley, H. (2003). Forward. In H. Beazley, J. Beggs, & L. C. Spears (Eds.), *The servant-leader within: A transformative path* (pp. 1–11). New York: Paulist Press.

Ferch, S. R. (2003). *Servant-leadership, forgiveness, and social justice.* Indianapolis, IN: The Greenleaf Center for Servant-leadership.

Greenleaf, R. K. (1972). *Institution as servant.* Westfield, IN: Greenleaf Center.

Greenleaf, R. K. (1977). *Servant leadership: A journey into the nature of legitimate power and greatness.* New York: Paulist Press.

Hall, B. P. (1994). *Values shift: A guide to personal & organizational transformation.* Rockport, MA: Twin Lights.

Kellerman, B. (2008). *Followership: How followers are creating change and changing leaders.* Boston, MA: Harvard Business School Press. Retrieved from http://catdir.loc.gov/catdir/toc/ecip0724/2007031572.html

Krulak, C. (2000). *Remarks at joint services conference on professional ethics.* Retrieved February 19, 2012, from http://www.appleseeds.org/krulak_integrity.htm

Lennick, D., & Kiel, F. (2005). *Moral intelligence: Enhancing business performance & Leadership success.* Upper Saddle River, NJ: Pearson Education Wharton School.

Michel, K. L. (2014). *Maslow's Hierarchy of Needs informed by Blackfoot Nation (Alta).* Retrieved 2015 from https://lincolnmichel.wordpress.com/2014/04/19/maslows-hierarchy-connected-to-blackfoot-beliefs/

Morelli, M. D., & Morelli, E. A. (Eds.). (2002). *The Lonergan reader.* Toronto: University of Toronto Press.

Scharmer, O., & Kaufer, K. (2013). *Leading from the emerging future: From ego-system to eco-system economies.* San Francisco: Barrett-Koehler.

Zohar, D., & Marshall, I. (2004). *Spiritual capital: Wealth we can live by.* San Francisco: Barrett-Koehler.

5

Listen-First Seeking Clarity Before Influence

Listening-First

Robert K. Greenleaf wrote and taught more extensively on listening than any other Servant-leader attribute, claiming we might "…become a natural servant through a long arduous discipline of learning to listen, a discipline sufficiently sustained that the automatic response to any problem is to listen first" (Greenleaf, 1977, p. 10). Servant-leaders in training come to realize that deep listening is a learned skill and a challenging discipline that calls forth a humble authenticity. Our ability to open up to the perspective of others and listen and be humbly present and available creates an interior space within ourselves for internal and external listening that in turn helps engender an environment hospitable to listening-first. Sincere and deliberate listening is a creative and influential act that potentially nurtures greater mutual wholeness.

Our capacity to hear is one of the first senses that develops as we form in the womb; likewise, hearing is often the last of the sensory systems to shut down when dying. Listening is a primary survival system. It is a capacity that is influenced by our wellness and our attentiveness. Changing the quality of our listening attentiveness seems to change the

© The Author(s) 2018
J. H. Horsman, *Servant-Leaders in Training*,
Palgrave Studies in Workplace Spirituality and Fulfillment,
https://doi.org/10.1007/978-3-319-92961-3_5

quality of our wellness and our consciousness. We can enhance our authenticity by learning to listen-first. Listening is not just about hearing sounds or understanding words, it also involves a choice to intentionally attend to what we hear and that involves learning to listen more profoundly or holistically such that our awareness is enhanced and our understanding enriched.

Listening is foundational to all forms of leadership communication. When compared with the importance of learning to write, read, and speak, listening is consistently identified as the most important skill for communication and learning (Janusik, Fullenkamp, & Partese, n.d.). Unsurprisingly, there is no lack of scientific knowledge on listening; over the last 100 years, scientists have learned much about listening and how to improve it. Ways of listening have been well researched and categorized; yet surprisingly, listening knowledge and skills are not well passed on in our formal education and leadership training programs. Considering all our communication skills, listening is the least taught, the least systematically learned, and effectively practiced. Generally, we receive much prescriptive instruction, but little actual training on how to listen.

There is a continuum of listening that extends from zero listening through to respectful and empathetic listening to deep generative listening. Categories of not listening include ignoring, pretending, controlling, and projecting. Ignoring is simply not listening or dismissing what the speaker (writer) is saying. Pretending is ignoring with the pretense of listening. People who pretend to listen communicate that listening is not their primary focus and are often experienced as dismissive to the speaker. Controlling is coercing or manipulating what the speaker says through body gestures, facial expressions, or vocal sounds. Have you attempted to speak to a person in authority and experienced feeling slightly inadequate (thrown off, or shamed), and ended up saying what you thought the listener wanted to hear, fudging the original message? When we edit a message as we speak, we may be attempting to deliver information that appears expressively disagreeable to a controlling recipient. Projecting is responding with our interpretation of what is being spoken, rejecting what the speaker is actually stating. When we project, we hear through our own filtering system of knowledge, judgments, biases, and perspectives; and while projecting, we may also be conveying our judgment of the person speaking. Another facet of projecting is our tendency to finish the speaker's statement, or we feel compelled to correctively restate the sentence how we perceive it should be stated. Another example of projecting occurs when we offer a preemptive response, concluding what the message means before it has been fully stated. Presumably, these examples of not listening and poor listening are familiar to us all. (See Table 5.1— Poor listening showing a continuum of listening from ignoring to the beginnings of effective listening.)

It seems that a very common listening practice is to *listen to respond as soon as possible*. Indeed, *listening to interject ASAP* seems to be a current listening strategy. It is a strategy that listens for bits of information, for facts, for points of agreement and disagreement, filtering out presumed useless information, attempting to capture valued information for analysis and synthesis within our knowledge base. Without doubt, such an approach may be effective listening in some situations, such as in an emergency and when time is of the essence. More often, in our urgency to listen to respond, we may unconsciously (or consciously) end up competing with colleagues to offer our perspective first, to win our point, to express our judgment, to show our brilliance, rather than seeking to discover the brilliance of the other. Sound familiar? This is the norm for many corporate, educational, and community cultures. In our efforts to get attention, recognition, and assert our status, we are often not really present or available to the whole of what a speaker is saying. As a result, we reveal a lack of authenticity, and in many instances, we apply very selective listening to what is being said, limiting our learning potential, and in so doing we often subtly, or blatantly, display our disrespect for others. A *listen to respond as soon as possible* strategy reveals our attitudinal disposition toward listening.

Table 5.1 A continuum of poor listening

```
-Ignoring—
         Pretending—
                   Controlling—
                             Projecting—
                                       Downloading—
                                                 Listening to Interject ASAP-->
```

Similar to serving-first, a listening-first strategy reveals a Servant-leader disposition.

We can change the world by learning to listen. Practicing and learning how to more effectively listen nurtures a healing and creative learning attitude. Such an attitude assumes that when we listen, the other will strive to creatively resolve their own issues and in doing so discover more of their own wholeness. Listening-first is a way to call forth others, it is a way of listening that allows others to be creative and reveal their own voice. Greenleaf's approach to listening was not about waiting for the right moment to interject our wisdom, or solve a problem, but to intentionally and expectantly await insight, illumination, and resolution to emerge from the other—as well as from within oneself. Listening with the intention that the speaker has the capacity to resolve the issue does not mean that the listener is discouraged from being present or responding, but rather that we are present and available in a way different from the strategy of interjecting as soon as possible. A listen-first strategy is a way that is supportive, collaborative, focused on learning as opposed to jockeying to download, score points, or debate. Learning to listen with a learning focus is respectful, engaging, and can be mutually creative. The kind of healing and transforming listening Greenleaf proposed invites co-creative listening; this kind of listening extends to forms of generative listening that may merge with generative dialog.

Numerous reports from organizations reveal that people yearn to have someone in leadership just listen to them and show that they understand, or at least care. Nurturing a desire to listen involves developing a different attitudinal capacity for listening, a capacity that is open to authentic, other-oriented, creative, holistic, and integrative listening experiences for both the speaker and the listener. Deeper listening facilitates a mutually enhancing collaborative generative learning dynamic. When a mutual search for greater understanding is manifest, a relational creative synergy may occur between individuals and within an entire group.

Listening is key to hearing and speaking with clarity. In a sense, listening-first is exercising a form of withdrawal that allows healing, creative learning, and wisdom to arise in the listener. In practice when we listen interiorly, we can be aware of our thoughts, our feelings, our sensing, and we may draw insights from the deeper depths of our interior.

When we intentionally listen to another, or with a group, our personal and collective listening capacity may intensify. Collective listening may open us to a creative collective wisdom. Learning to listen internally as well as externally involves integrating more holistic listening awareness into our servant-consciousness, and that may influence the listening quality of our collective consciousness.

Listen-first is very engaging, we self-monitor while oscillating between choosing to keep quiet and speaking. Interiorly, while listening and waiting for a speaker to articulate and think through what they are saying, we learn to attend to our own rational inconsistencies, make insightful connections and corrections as the other continues to speak. Doing this takes patience and humility on the part of the listener. Listening is especially challenging when an appropriate solution is obvious to the listener. Learning to listen in this way engenders humility, especially when we suspend our desire to offer our knowledge in favor of allowing the creative intelligence of the speaker to emerge. Our humility may be even more deeply tested when the speaker comes up with a brilliant solution we had never considered—a solution that may never have emerged if we had not been listening. The experience of deliberately attending to our listening often reveals just how inattentive we actually are, and this awareness can be a starting point to our learning to humbly listen more effectively.

Greenleaf (1996) made a remarkable claim about healing and listening, "Great as I believe the healing power of listening to be upon the one [who speaks], a much greater healing takes place with one who learns and assiduously practices listening" (p. 95). Greenleaf's insight implies listening is not only mutually beneficial, the greater benefit of listening-first is healing and creative learning for the listener. Greenleaf's salient point implies that in order to listen with a serving-first capacity, one has to be humbly open to learning and being influenced by the other. The point also affirms that the motive for listening-first is similar if not synonymous with the profoundly relational motive for Servant-leading. Greenleaf's insight has implications for leadership training and development programs, as a listening-first disposition may influence a more synergistic holistic way of learning for oneself and others.

Admittedly, modeling serving-first listening is challenging. It is extremely challenging to intentionally practice and sustain a listening-first approach in our fast-paced, high-demand, results-oriented corporate organizational cultures. Listening-first involves a fundamental attitudinal shift in our listening purpose and focus, a focus that communicates an authentic desire to be present and available to the speaker—and that cannot be easily faked. A listening-first approach calls for patience, humility, a tolerance for diverse views, as well as a respect for the dignity of other people, all of which require learning new value priorities for listening. A listening-first capacity involves striving for a more holistic listening awareness, respectful influence, the practice of discernment, and a preference for generative listening and generative dialog.

Toward Holistic Listening

Our capacity for listening reflects our state of being, such that changing the quality of our listening changes the dispositional quality of our being and at times our very identity. When our heart, head, body and spirit are in harmony, others somehow know or sense this, and our mutual communications gain clarity and may become more holistic. Holistic listening involves trusting that nothing will be lost or forgotten, trusting that mutual hearing and understanding is occurring, and trusting that when the opportunity is ripe, the knowing will emerge as an insight, or as a profound act, or as words of wisdom. Learning to listen holistically begins with respectful empathetic listening and moves toward forms of generative listening and generative dialog.

A framework for holistic listening is drawn from the writings of the Jesuit philosopher Bernard Lonergan. In his work *Insight*, Lonergan proposed some operative criteria that underlie how humans *come to know* (Lonergan in Morelli & Morelli, 2002). Lonergan's writings are an in-depth philosophical exploration of many aspects of the human condition that drive far beyond listening. Nonetheless, Lonergan's description of how humans *come to know* is a helpful contextual model (metaphor) for elaborating Greenleaf's holistic approach to listening. Lonergan offers a structure that serves as a framework to help us understand how intentionally attending to our listening may help build capacity for more holistic listening.

Lonergan's structure consists of four innate transcendental principles of intentionality that inherently promote self-growth, authenticity, and progress for all humans (Lonergan in Morelli & Morelli, 2002, p. 22). Lonergan's four principles are *be attentive, be intelligent, be reasonable*, and *be responsible*. These constructs operate as intentions in "the spontaneous, structural dynamism of human consciousness" at the level of sensory experience, the level of coming to understand, the level of judgment, and the level of decision and action (p. 22). Lonergan emphasized that the focus and qualities of intentionality and consciousness differ at each successive level. Although the functionality of the transcendental operators cannot be broken apart—they are a dynamic structure; however, each can be intentionally attended to (otherwise they would never have been identified as such).

At the sensory level of experience, we are consciously or unconsciously attentive; we continuously sense our environment, we perceive, feel, hear, and move using our perceptive organic and psychic monitoring systems. The second successive level involves making the sensed data intelligible: we question, sort, imagine, gain insight, and come to understand what we are perceiving, and consciously express in thought and language what we have understood, and formatively work out the implications of our impressions and expressions. The third level, reasoning and judging, involves drawing on our experience and understandings; we reflect, organize the evidence, and pass judgment on the logic, the truth or falsity, certainty or probability of an experience or idea. The decision level intends responsible action, applying our informed (or misinformed) perception, deliberating and evaluating options, deciding and carrying out our decisions (Lonergan in Morelli & Morelli, 2002, pp. 448–450).

Listening occurs simultaneously through these four qualitatively different dynamic functionalities; how might we use them to help explore a more holistic approach to listening? To begin with, being attentive *sensing* and being intelligent *intelligibility making* are the first two activities of the dynamics of *coming to know*. Sensing is where we take in the perceptible data through noticing, feeling, hearing, and moving. The second level where unconscious data is transformed into conscious intelligibility is where the sensory data is made understandable through inquiry, insights, striving to understand and express what we have understood, and working through the reasonableness of our impressions is a pathfinder aspect of consciousness. The first two levels reveal why listening is so important; this is where impressions are formed and understanding begins. The second level is where the data is most raw and most available for interpretive and holistic and creative listening.

Regarding the principles *be reasonable* and *be responsible*, it is interesting that our Western education systems, from primary school right through higher education, have focused almost exclusively on developing these higher order capacities of rationalizing and judging, and decision and implementing. As educators, we have become very good at teaching how to analyze, synthesize and rationalize, judge, make decisions, and implement. Humanity has progressed much from these efforts; however, there is more to learn. We now can enrich our knowledge and learning by intentionally attending to the more unconscious processes *be attentive* and *be intelligent*. The good news is that our education systems have shown that we have a capacity to attend to each of the two higher order functions, so implicitly we also have the capacity to learn how to attend to sensing and intelligibility making. A task for the Servant-leader in training is to further draw into consciousness how to *be intelligent* and *be attentive*.

Figure 5.1 depicts a metaphor for holistic listening. Lonergan's four transcendental operators for *coming to know* are represented along with approximations of our data filtering process. Notice that information filtering begins during the intelligibility making operation (if not before) and continues throughout the reasoning, judging, and decision operations. Note that our unconscious sensory capacity absorbs as much as 11 million bits of raw information per second; however, the capacity of our conscious mind cannot exceed 40 bits of information per second. Most of the time, the conscious mind is operating with about 16 bits of information per second (Data Filtering, QURA, 2016). For the most part, much of this filtering process seems to occur at the unconscious level, and the bulk of the data filtering process may occur during the intelligibility making process.

Is it possible to become more aware of our sensory and intelligibility making process by merely attending to it, and how might we by pass or somehow suspend our automatic filtering process? It seems reasonable that the more attentive we are to our sensory (data) gathering systems,

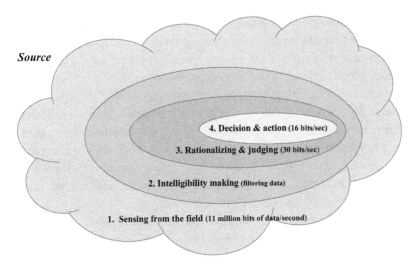

Source

4. Decision & action (16 bits/sec)

3. Rationalizing & judging (30 bits/sec)

2. Intelligibility making (filtering data)

1. Sensing from the field (11 million bits of data/second)

Fig. 5.1 Awareness, listening, and filtering. Holistic listening: learning to intentionally attend to each transcendental capacity. Learning to attend to sensing and intelligibility making (disrupting filtering) may enhance awareness

the more likely we are to become more directly aware of what is being sensed. Similarly, if we learn to attend to our intelligible listening, we may be able to become aware of and temporarily influence our filtering process by suspending our judgments and biases and opening ourselves to the field of sensory data. By doing that we may open opportunities for more insights, awareness, and access to new data, in addition to what we already know. In turn, that should enhance our capacity to rationalize and make good judgments and better decisions. Suspending our judgments and opening ourselves to more listening is in itself a more holistic endeavor.

Holistic listening begins with listening to our listening. The Benedictine monk Basil Pennington (2000) suggested we might become more adept at holistic listening by attending to our capacity to listen to our listening. Just as we use our ears to listen for sound, similarly we use our eyes to listen for color and perspective, our nose for scent, and our mouth for all kinds of tastes (pp. 22–25). Pennington suggested that our whole being is a sensing organism, and our sensory gathering system can be channeled through our capacity for listening. By being attentive, even our inner faculties can be more finely tuned to listen for emotions, memories, images, insights, ideas, and concepts. In other words, we have the capacity to enhance our awareness of our whole outer and inner sensory listening system simply by learning to intentionally attend to our listening capacities.

To enhance our listening awareness, Pennington (2000) suggests we might begin by realistically acknowledging our current listening capacity (and this may occur at any point in time) that awareness point can then become a benchmark for improving our listening. Such that, during the listening process whenever we become aware that our attentiveness has diminished, we may choose to renew our focus. While listening, we may find ourselves needing to refocus our attention, and the quality of our presence, several times in the span of a few minutes (or even a few seconds). Doing this affirms that we have the awareness and the ability to intentionally attend to our listening.

Intentionally attending to our listening is a discipline that requires practice to learn. Attending to our listening is primarily an interior focus, but it also involves listening exteriorly. Learning the discipline can be experientially enhanced with empathetic listing and more profoundly through generative listening and generative dialog with others. Assuredly, intentional attending to our listening will draw some of our formerly unconscious activities into our experiential awareness and into our conscious functioning.

In our efforts to develop a profoundly relational, creative, holistic, and integrative servant-consciousness, we can learn to embrace a more holistic approach to listening. Using a listening-first approach of intentionally attending to our listening, we may become more conscious, more aware of our listening and what we are hearing and sensing; this in itself is more holistic listening. By being more present, more attentive to what we are hearing, seeing, feeling, with another person, we in turn may also stimulate and affirm a more attentive presence within the other person, creating the potential for enhanced mutual empathetic awareness and learning. (Learning to enhance our sensory and intelligibility making skills is further addressed within the topic of presencing in the Chap. 6, on "Pathfinding-Foresight.")

Greater integration of the cognitive mind and heart–body–mind is likely to be a holistic integrative outcome of the developmental shift from 1st Tier to 2nd Tier development. The heart–brain is sometimes described as the (mostly unconscious) rhythmic system. Researchers at the *HeartMath Institute* suggest that the heart–mind is continually developing and influences all our interactions with everyone and everything. The heart has 60 times greater electrical voltage amplitude and a 5000 times stronger magnetic field than that produced by the cognitive brain. Heart awareness is multiple times faster than the cognitive brain and the rhythmic chronologically develops prior to the brain. Human brains are not just located in the skull, the human brain is a holistic heart–body sensory system (McCraty, Bradly, & Tomasino, n.d.). "Research shows that the heart does in fact literally think, feel, and remember; is formed and nurtured; by and connects with other hearts" (Pearsall, 2007, p. 2). If you place a live heart cell on or beside other live body cells, it would not be long before the body cells are beating in rhythm with the heart cell (p. 3). Speculatively, what does that tell us? The heart is profoundly relational: Servant-leading is profoundly relational.

Developing a servant-consciousness involves developing our awareness of heart-consciousness. Heart-consciousness involves stimulating a more integrated relational awareness. Shifting our center of awareness from primarily the cognitive to include greater awareness of the head, heart, and body implies bringing our relational, intelligibility making, and sensing capacities into greater conscious awareness. In addition to our heart, our bodies seem to hold and/or be able to access wisdom. Gandhi (1913) stated, "We but mirror the world. All the tendencies present in the outer world are to be found in the world of our body. If we could change ourselves, the tendencies in the world would also change. As a man changes his own nature, so does the attitude of the world change towards him" (p. 124). Learning to listen holistically is in part about allowing the heart–body sensory system to metaphorically and sometimes literally speak directly to us and teach us about our human nature.

Generative Listening

Holistic listening emerges from a listening-first strategy. A listening-first strategy seems to reside on a continuum that begins with respectful listening and ranges through variations of generative listening. Respectful listening is foundational to hearing the content of a communication and responding to what is actually being stated. Respectful listening implies being present to the speaker, being engaged and receptive, and communicating our understanding. Leading from an authentic relational commitment engenders a *there I am also* perspective. A *there I am also* perspective engenders respect, compassion, and humility and a desire to authentically generously serve with gratitude and joy. Table 5.2 shows that respectful listening leads to deeper levels of empathetic and generative listening which in turn aid discernment, generative dialog, and influential persuasion.

From respectful listening, we move toward empathetic listening. Empathetic listening is mutually engaging. It involves reflecting and experiencing other people's feelings and states of being through a quality of presence that helps the speaker see themselves with more clarity, even in the silences between our words. Listening with empathy involves striving to hear the intention behind the content with sincerity and respect, attempting to view the situation from the speaker's point of view, listening for content and what is being asked within their values and purpose, and what is not being verbalized. It also involves observation and constant approximation and adjustment of our understanding, as we listen to hear rather than answer, waiting for the speaker to finish, thinking about how we might respond, and judging the accuracy of the speaker's words. Empathizing enables us to respond by aiding the other person's intention; this is done by attempting to see the whole picture and respond with the intention of preserving and continuing the relationship.

Moving to generative listening involves attending to the deep silence within as we creatively listen to hear and comprehend the meaning of what we hear, feel, and see being spoken around us. As Pennington suggested, we become a finely tuned receiver that picks up what currently is

Table 5.2 Toward holistic listening

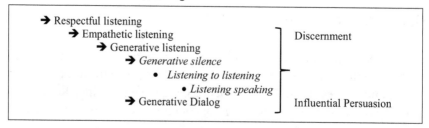

and what wants to be communicated. To do this we need a relational commitment to serving-first and listening-first and be open to tuning our sensory system to the other's purpose. In generative listening often something uniquely new is stimulated: an insight, a new idea, a new awareness, or a more comprehensive understanding of an issue. Generative listening involves listening with our whole being, such that it seems we are connected to something larger than ourselves, and we often experience a resolving (rather than chaotic) flow of creative energy. We have a sense of being attuned not only to the present but also with a deeper realm of emerging presence where intention and action come as one, and we catch a glimpse or experience of communion with something greater than ourselves (Scharmer & Kaufer, 2013). Questions and more holistic solutions that we had not considered before may simply emerge, in part, because our judgments and biases are being held in abeyance, as we patiently attend to what is emerging unthreatened by differences of opinion or worldviews.

Generative silence, listening to listening, listening speaking, and generative dialog may emerge within generative listening. Some find silence uncomfortable, at times oppressive, but with accepting patience and some endurance we may find that beneath the resistance is a level of tranquility that welcomes the silences. As an aspect of holistic listening, listening to silence also includes learning to listen to wisdom within the silence.

> Each of us have an ever-faithful companion-presence…this companion-presence is Silence (p. 7)…Our body's center is the necessary meeting point where the inward silence of solitude meets up with the great Silence of Cosmic Wisdom. When we do not cultivate this meeting point in the right ways, we lose access to our soul, to the presence of the Silence, and to our individual place in the Wisdom of the World (p. 8). Silence…is a mode, a form of intelligence. It is wisdom. As we enter into Silence, we enter into Wisdom. We do not become wise but enter into the objective Wisdom of world processes…as we enter into the Wisdom of Silence, we allow ourselves to be taught by the things of the world. (Sardello, 2008, p. 81)

Not only are we able to learn from silence, we also learn to conceptualize and teach from the emerging wisdom through generative dialog.

Generative silence (listening to silence) is a very powerful form of relational engagement. Respecting silence may heighten our sense of presence. Periods of silence can open us up to more sensitive listening. We may listen interiorly for what wants to speak, or what to speak, and for the right moment to speak it, or continue to remain silent—even when it feels uncomfortable.

Sometimes silence speaks more than words; at times it is the best way to communicate empathy, agreement, or unanimity. It requires the listener's utmost level of attention, presence, and intention. Sometimes generative silences aid our ability to access and speak wisdom. Also, by remaining silent and attending to the person speaking, we may help them access deeper aspects within themselves (a form of focusing).

At times generative listening can be experienced as co-creative. For example, an aspect of generative listening is called listening to listening. Listening to listening has an internal and an external focus. Attentive speakers are aware of how their speaking is received while they speak. While listening to listening, we become aware of how others are hearing us, and that awareness influences our internal listening and how we are speaking. While listening to listening, we may tailor what is being said to the audience's capacity for understanding. In this sense our listening is not about changing our talk to say what the listeners want to hear; rather, it is about tailoring what we are saying for the greater clarity of the listeners. Listening to listening is a way of serving the listener by letting the audiences need for understanding speech through the speaker, in such a way that the listener in a sense gains a voice and in gaining that voice reaches greater comprehension of what is being spoken.

Sardello (2008) described a nuance of this subtle internal listening to listening as speaking–listening (I prefer to call it listening-speaking). When we listen deeply while we are speaking, we can intentionally attend to the silence between words. When doing this, we can become aware of the words we are saying as we create them, of the way the words feel as they emerge within our sensing body, of the stream of semi-formed thoughts and emotions out of which our words are coming, and of the receptive group space into which we are offering them; this is listening to our speaking. Listening-speaking is a generative process, such that we may find ourselves creatively conceptualizing words and noticing that a word doesn't quite feel right internally, or doesn't accurately express the experience, or is not precise enough for the situation, and we find ourselves recalling that word, while searching within for a more accurate articulation that is more clarifying to the external listeners. Listening-speaking in this way is an example of authentic communication that is in tune with what needs to be said at a given time. When a group is listening-speaking, they are in generative dialog, and healing and creative learning may arise as truths and wisdom.

Generative listening and generative dialog are creating through emergence. Creating through emergence is quite different from a rational insight or brainstorming. The generative process is other engaging in the sense that it could not be done without awareness and engagement with the other (the collective). What arises is created together and is often slowly and awkwardly pulled from space. Like reeling in a hooked fish from the depths of the ocean, we really do not know what kind it is, or how big it is, and we have to work it and attend to it, as it comes to the surface. We really do not know what we have hooked onto until it is in the boat. And even then we may not be able to identify it exactly because we have never seen this fish before, all we know is that, now, it is in our boat, and we need to examine it and learn from it.

We know we are experiencing generative listening and generative dialog when we notice that in the flow of listening and dialog, we are struggling to creatively articulate what we are sensing and feeling. We may be healing the old and while creating something new, birthing a new idea or a new identity as we speak. Often the dialog with others slows down, as other members of the group find themselves creatively conceptualizing along with us, sometimes ahead of us, sometimes behind us, certainly along with us, creatively serving a more holistic conceptualization of what wants to be expressed. This creative process is experienced as a resolving invigorating collective flow; it is like pulling a fish from the pool of collective wisdom. When we experience generativity in these ways, we are likely accessing *collective wisdom*. Collective wisdom may arise when a *Generative Wisdom Structure* is active such as *I–You–We–It* which can be described as first person, second person, third person, and It (Nature, Spirit, and Source). When this structure is evoked, generative listening and generative dialog involve attunement with cognitive, personal, and empathetic (relational) feelings, as well as sensory awareness.

Generative listening is informing and creative; there seems to be an inherent creative and transforming impulse within generativity. Generative dialog is informing and creative with others. The variations of generative listening and generative dialog reveal our capacity for intensely meaningful, creative, life-changing communication. Whether occurring interiorly within our self, like the silent conversation that can happen between an artist and the viewer of the artist's work, or interiorly and exteriorly with others, generative listening and generative dialog affirm a greater sense of wholeness. Generative listening, listening to listening, and speaking–listening are inherently dialogic. Generative dialog is profoundly relational, co-creative, holistic, and integrative. Generative dialog requires an intention to be present and available; it assumes a sense of safety and trust in the group and the will to heal and creatively learn through listening and speaking on meaningful issues. Generative dialog assumes we are somehow able to communicate with others on multiple levels, levels that penetrate words and their meaning, often at a deeper level than we generally are aware of or even cognitively intend, a level that is mutual relational creation in the moment. Developing one's ability to listen, be present, and empathize enhances one's awareness, and that in turn opens wide our lens of perception and opens us to creative generative dialog.

Relating this to the capacity for serving-first, it is apparent that the more we are authentically available to listen, receive data, and make it intelligible, and the more we strive to articulate our understanding of an issue, the more potential for healing, creative learning and enhanced individual, and mutual understanding and creativity. Generative engagement involves informing and inspiriting mind, heart, body holistically. Generative listening and generative dialog are profoundly relational and inherently creative and are in themselves ways of serving-first. Servant-leaders in training may further develop their capacity for listening by learning to listen more deeply in two realms, the internal and the external, in progressively more integrative and holistic ways. Authentic conversations within a group are potentially transforming, and experience affirms that the creativity that emerges from generative listening and dialog tends to generate systems thinking. Furthermore, generative listening and generative dialog enhance our capacity for more holistic discernment, and influential persuasion (see Fig. 5.2). By intentionally attending to ourselves and the listening in the room, our words may come to express a truer conceptualization of what is emerging not in a manipulative way but in a respectful influential persuasive way.

Discernment

"The only reality to be trusted is that which shelters decision-making with sensitivity and compassion so that one sees and feels what fits the situation, is the prompting of the human spirit—from the heart" (Greenleaf, 1977, p. 318). The developmental journey toward greater integrated awareness and wholeness is perhaps the greatest human adventure, and this journey lies before each of us. An important aspect of the journey is that we all have an inner self that yearns to be known and congruently integrated with our exterior self. Learning to trust the heart involves learning a language to speak about the interior experience. A method for learning the language of the mind, heart, and will is called discernment. Discerning is away to practice attending to our will, our emotions, and our reason to get at a deeper more holistic awareness of what seems right for us, or a group. Reason, feelings, and our will are always involved in discerning a good decision, and as such discernment is a holistic integrative process.

There are many fine resources available on the topic of discernment; the intention of this brief is to provide a complementary frame of reference for a holistic listening and decision-making approach. St. Ignatius of Loyola developed a form of discernment that helps weigh the spiritual influences on our will, feelings, and reason. Learning the practice of discernment is about learning to listen interiorly to three kinds of inner movements within our self and others. The Ignatian exercises are practices that help discerners sort through the natural inclinations of will, and feelings, and integrate those with reason to help make more holistically informed decisions. Ignatian discernment is a language and a methodology for learning to attend to our interior life and using the method helps integrate our inner knowing with judging, making decisions, and acting in the world.

A discernment process is most useful when we are faced with major transitions. Transitions call forth questions of identity—who I am, what is my purpose, and what is most meaningful—and these are always in motion or yearning to be in motion. Transitions seem to require at least some struggle, sometimes transitions entail trudging through prolonged agony, but experience shows there always seems to be a beginning, a middle, and an end to these processes. Discernment involves developing a capacity for internal listening, awareness, and the learning of a descriptive language for our interior experiences. When we become adept at discernment, we find ourselves energized and inspired and, as a result, experience more life-enriching decisions and actions, even in the face of many obstacles. Discernment is about attending to our senses, intelligibility making, and reasoning so we can make better judgments and in the process build capacity for better decision-making.

Discernment always involves making a choice between good and feasible options. Options may be examined using three modes (kinds) of discernment (Sparough, Manney, & Hipskind, 2010). Mode One is an overwhelming certainty that one of the options being considered is the right one. There is no doubt about which is the right and appropriate choice. All that is left to do is decide. Mode Two is applicable when we are emotionally conflicted between options. In this mode, we learn to sift through our feelings seeking consolation and/or desolation in search of peace and affirmation around one option. If consolation does not occur and desolation prevails, then we seek more information and take more time. We do not make a decision. Mode Three involves calm deliberation and reasoning. When there is no clear rightness about an option, and there does not seem to be a lot of emotional involvement, then just look at the facts pragmatically and weigh the advantages and disadvantages of each option and make a preliminary decision seeking consolation or desolation. The three modes of discernment are differentiated to emphasize that the intuitive will, sorting through feelings, and reasoning are all involved in making good decisions.

No mode is superior to the other. Each mode will be present in a decision process, while one is likely to be more prevalent in a specific circumstance. Sometimes an insight has a rightness (Mode One), but is very rough and unclear; our feelings around the insight may help us sort out some of the clarity; and inevitably the insight may need to be presented as a rational logical idea. We can learn to attend to the different modes, and that is what we are attempting to learn with the discernment exercises.

Becoming aware of our feelings is part of developing emotional intelligence (EQ). We have the capacity to observe our feelings and not get caught up in them. We can learn that there is a variety of emotions and that some emotions are not even ours. Discernment involves learning to sort through these feelings and pay attention to the emotions that console us and those that leave us feeling desolate or fragmented. Suffering seems to be associated with desolation. A feeling of desolation is a sign of incongruity. Sometimes we need to identify and acknowledge the focus of the desolation and let go, or heal it, before we can move on. Sometimes the desolation is not internal, but rather is felt as time pressure, or is felt as a projection of someone else's emotions or control. Clarifying the internal or external source of the emotions is part of the discernment process that can be liberating in the sense that it frees us to act out of our own sense of rightness. Developing awareness of the subtleties of these movements takes humility and practice: this is as much an interior spiritual process as it is physical, emotional, and cognitive; all are involved, and all help us assume responsibility for our decisions.

The Ignatian exercises teach us to become more aware of our experience by attending to the feeling when we identify with what affirms us. When our desires and choices are affirmed internally and externally by others, we feel consolation; this is the counterpart to the feeling of desolation. We can learn to recognize pride and self-importance as desolation; our soul knows the difference between forms of pride and authentic desire in our efforts to discern the greater deeper good in our decisions.

Developing a servant-consciousness is about drawing on a more expansive and inclusive awareness centered in discernment of the heart, mind, and will. It is not about one capacity overriding or excluding another (mind over heart, or self-willing it), it is about creatively striving for a harmonious, integrated wholeness. The human spirit speaks through our deep feelings and our will as well as our rationality. The three modes are all aspects of a more holistic approach to making decisions. Enhancing our awareness and disposition toward listening and discerning is a primary area of influence in Servant-leader formation and is a way to grow our servant-consciousness.

Influential Persuasion

How often do we reflect on the personal effects and costs of coercion? Greenleaf wrote "coercive power is useful to stop something or destroy something, but not much constructive can be done with it" (1995, p. 25). Elsewhere he wrote "coercion is not in any way synonymous with leadership" (2003, p. 73). Many of us have become numb to how much we are coerced and manipulated; yet, we all know what coercion and manipulation feels like when it is blatantly applied to us, and more subtly we know at a deep level how we feel when we are coercing others. As we become more aware of coercion and manipulation, we may find our self quite disturbed. For example, it has often occurred to me that the motivational carrot has in reality just been the orange end of the same stick of *threats and fear*. For many today, the word manipulation has a negative connotation, the result perhaps of too much inappropriate control and inauthentic and inappropriate behavior modification.

When attempting to alter the perspective of others, often our automatic strategy is to use our power to force, manipulate, and coerce. With awareness, we realize we have another choice, and we can choose to listen for clarity then influence and persuade. Manipulation is a method of imposing our will on others, whereas a desire to influence conveys respect and engages and invites the other to use their own genius and develop their own opinion. With exception of some aspects of parenting, when we impose our view, we are not really concerned about the other person; rather, it is about our view over theirs. Unsurprisingly, imposing our will is often resisted and resented and is detrimental to the relationship. Greenleaf (1998) indicated that being persuaded is something that happens when we arrive at a decision using our own intuitive sense, as opposed to having someone force an idea on us.

The language and actions of the Servant-leader are grounded in a fundamental respect for the dignity of the human person, and that respect becomes the heart of all relationships. To not be gentle with others implies that we are likely not being gentle with ourselves, and that lacks respect on both counts. Our authenticity (integrity) speaks louder than our words, and when we speak out of our authenticity, it is possible to be gentle and firm at the same time.

A formidable barrier to listening and discerning more holistically is our bias for rational reasoning. The bias assumes our capacity to reason is superior to feelings, emotions, and yearnings of the will; however, listening-first draws out more enriched information when we attend to listening with all of our faculties. Nevertheless, it seems easier and preferable for those of us trained in rational logic to use it exclusively when dealing with relationship issues, foregoing the knowing that we are all living feeling spiritual beings. As leaders, as parents, as friends, we at times find ourselves morally obligated to interfere with other people's lives. Yet, Greenleaf called for a form of persuasion that does not include manipulation or coercion (see Table 5.3).

Influential persuasion is not part of the power continuum (Greenleaf, 1977). For the Servant-leader persuasion is completely free of coercion and manipulation: persuasion occurs when we freely arrive at a decision based on what we know and our own intuition. Greenleaf's call for persuasion without coercion or manipulation is counterintuitive to the autocrat and the manager; he is calling forth a different disposition, one guided by compassion and generosity supported by skills and behaviors such as respect, authenticity, integrity, trust, and humility. These values do not mean that we do not speak the truth; on the contrary, we speak the truth with profound respect. Truth like wisdom carries its own grace, such that most people prefer it and are able to accept it. Servant-leaders in training strive to speak their truths in a way that has the most potential to be listened to, and acknowledged.

Influential persuasion assumes that our power to influence arises from a commitment to serve-first, from a commitment to independence–interdependence, and a willingness to be authentic, present, and available. In other words our attitudinal disposition, who we are, will determine what gets addressed and how. Influential persuasion calls for a responsible moral approach to leading. Gentle (respectful) persistent persuasion is less likely to produce resistance and may invite dialog, aware healing, and creative learning.

The Servant-leader in training practices negotiating conflict in positive ways, ways that do not destroy relationships, ways that preserve relational stability. Striving to view conflict constructively can challenge us to the

Table 5.3 Influential persuasion

Power and Influence	
Power Continuum 1st Tier (primarily)	Influence Continuum 2nd Tier (primarily)
-Coercion------Manipulation------Persuasion-|	--*Influential Persuasion*--
--*Influential Persuasion is effective through each Stage of development*--	

Greenleaf's notions of power and influential persuasion

core of our identity, especially when it is a personal attack from those close to us. Yet, Servant-leaders seldom do everything perfect—we are in training. Conflict is normal, and Servant-leaders will find themselves in no less conflict than anyone else; they may even find themselves in more conflict, as they struggle to reveal incongruent system values. System adaptation is seldom easy, and conceptualizing new views is often awkward and difficult, especially when others are resisting, not listening, or downloading what has always worked in the past. What Servant-leaders strive not to do is coerce, control, manipulate, and abuse.

Dialog is not a discussion, or a debate. Dialog assumes a free flow of thought and feelings between people. The Greeks considered dialog (a conversation with a flow of meaning) vital to self-governance. Once a society loses the capacity to respectfully dialog, all that is left is discussion. Discussion is about breaking apart what others say for the purpose of winning our point (Senge, 1995, p. 228). Attempting to influence persuasively without coercion or manipulation invites respectful dialog. Dialog may arise from empathetic and generative listening. Through dialog, we strive to become both teacher and learner.

A question all leaders should ponder is how do we get to an *I–You* relationship? Generative dialog is an effective way to bring about deep motivational shifts and resulting behavioral changes in a group, or an organizational culture. Generative dialog helps us to discover, articulate, bring to the surface, and challenge the assumptions that support our motives and our incongruities. Dialog can lead to a change in our existing paradigms, our mental models.

As Servant-leaders in training, we are encouraged to strive to raise communication above that of a competitive debate, or a discussion. The leader's role is to model and help facilitate dialog. Congruent modeling has a powerful impact in times of adversity and conflict. Somehow others know when we are modeling consistency and authenticity. When we fall short, as Servant-leaders we ask for forgiveness and offer forgiveness to others. Forgiveness reveals integrity and reinforces our sense of humility. Servant-leaders in training see others as necessary contributors to resolving conflict.

Questions are one of the better ways to stimulate a dialog; however, questions can be crafted to control and shut people down as well as open up dialog. Questions are subject to the attitudinal disposition of the questioner as well as the nature of the question itself. Questions designed to stimulate dialog may not necessarily do, as questions resonate with the interior condition of the speaker and also the receiver. If the receiver prefers to download, or debate, even the most well-intended and well-framed question may not lead to generative dialog. That being stated, getting to generative creative dialog is a mutual communal process that effective questioning may help facilitate. Authenticity, awareness, and a humble transparent desire to serve-first are helpful, and congruent modeling is a powerful way to influence, as building a respectful trusting relationship needs to occur and be ongoing within the group (see Fig. 4.2, Chap. 4).

Listening Spirals

Creating symbols and structures for our listening can influence the way we experience and think about listening. A galaxy spiral is by its structure always an open system. A *listening spiral* is a metaphor and a model of a galaxy spiral. A *listening spiral* is a structure for aware healing and creative learning, it requires an individual and others, it symbolizes natural and sacred space, and it is a representative pattern of creation. The listening spiral is a potent metaphor for generative listening and generative dialog.

Spirals are exceedingly symbolic: the more we study them, the more they resonate within the depths of our being. Spirals are patterns that penetrate the depths and breadths of nature, representing rhythmic, cyclic, motion, and flow. They can be seen as symbols of harmonious balance, integrated wholeness comprising inherent wisdom. The center of the spiral is the heart (the caldron, the crucible) of creative transformation that radiates and spins out new creations in an outward open expression of flow, while the gravitational spin of spiraling elements is also always drawing elements back toward the center. The outward flow and inward draw is symbolic of the arteries and the veins connecting our pumping heart, and of breathing out and breathing in, of healing and creative learning.

Most of us are familiar with the concept and function of talking circles. Talking circles can be healing and transformative for the speaker and the participants. The principles of the talking circle are mythically inspired by stories of King Arthur and the Knights of the Round Table, and by Quaker tradition, as well as Native American mythology. A *talking circle* is a forum to use (find) your voice, to speak your truths, and hopefully to be empathetically heard. A *talking circle* structures the priority of the gathering. Participants sit, or stand, in a rounded space facing each other. The circle is a structure that provides a forum that focuses on the speaker having the opportunity to give voice without interruption. The primary focus of a *talking circle* is speaking, and the secondary purpose is to listen and learn and perhaps come to a common understanding.

There can be problems with circles, circles may become closed systems, closed to new people, closed to new ideas, closed to a flexible organic flow; they can become self-serving systems. Also, when someone speaks, no one is necessarily obligated to listen, or respond. The prime responsibility rests with the speaker who temporarily controls the forum. In terms of the human development models, this tendency to close the circle arises within 1st Tier (Stages I and II) value systems, where worldviews are held to be mutually exclusive, where ego-centrism or ethno-centrism might keep the circle closed to those with different values and skills. When circles are closed, other worldviews are considered irrelevant, inferior, or threatening. To reduce the risk of closed system thinking, the circle should always remain open.

A profoundly relational, creative, holistic, and integrative organization or society might be built on some of the principles inherent in a spiral galaxy. Spirals are a natural configuration that form, unform, reform, and transform energy, elements, and life itself. Spirals are simple and complex and can be found throughout all of creation. On the earth, we see spiral formations in rocks, in water, in fire, in the air (storms), in plant growth, and in our experience of human growth and development. The galaxy spiral is a symbol of our home, our world, our solar system, our place in a galaxy among galaxies. A galaxy spiral is a relatively stable open system in perpetual transformation.

A listening spiral may be symbolic or actual (see Fig. 5.2). There is always a way in and another way out. It is an individual and collective space to practice holistic listening. Each round of the spiral signifies internal and external (micro, meso, macro, mundo) listening. A *listening spiral* has a dual purpose and a dual focus, to stimulate generative listening

Fig. 5.2 Galaxy spiral and listening spiral. A depiction of the Milky Way Galaxy. Printed with permission of Gonzaga University. Author's photo of a listening spiral

and generative dialog, it summons independence and interdependence. The name structures its primary purpose. Focusing our listening does not reduce the role or the importance of the speaker, as the role of the speaker is to listen interiorly and exteriorly stimulating generative listening and generative dialog. Adding to the focus of the speaker is the mutual responsibility of the listener to listen interiorly and generatively. The prime responsibility in a listening spiral is to listen holistically, thus the responsibility is shared equally with all. This mutual sharing of responsibility affirms the role of the individual and the collective. In this sense serving-first leadership is plural; both speaker and listener mutually serve each other and the collective.

Many of the principles of the talking circle also apply to a listening spiral with some important distinctions. While the speaker presents there is no debate, no one else speaks or interrupts; there is no cross talk or side conversation. These rules are foundational to the structure of respect. Deciding who will speak can be a subtle process, nuanced by rhythmic flow. For example, an experienced facilitator can read the group by listening to know who is ready, or who ought to speak next. Sometimes the collective consciousness spontaneously knows who ought to speak next, and that person is designated verbally or nonverbally. More simply, the next speaker may be chosen by the person who last spoke, or by a participant signaling readiness to speak. When the process goes around more than once, a natural resolving rhythmic flow emerges.

What is different about a *listening spiral* is its inherent openness. A spiral is inherently an open system; there is always a dual entry or exit: one way in and optionally another way out. Metaphorically we never leave the same (way) as we arrived. We exit somehow transformed or at least in a different state than when we entered. Additionally, having two ways to the center is symbolic of individual and collective actualization; both are necessary for both to flourish. The *independence–interdependence* dynamic is activated in that individual and collective creativity arises from people generatively listening and generatively speaking from their mind, heart, and will.

Learning to listen involves learning to gently surrender the numerous voices in our head: the voices of judgment and impatience; the voices of cynicism and doubt; the voices of fear and of self-abandonment; all of these must be continuously surrendered while we attend to the listening. While we are listening, we strive to catch the flow of insights and connections that flash in our mind and hold them in space, until we have time to give them a thorough acknowledgment, trusting providence that we will not forget them before the listening is done. Often, with *listening spirals*, we can get caught up in a flow of meaning and gain greater clarity as we spiral deeper in our listening, transforming our understanding in the flow.

The notion of a spiral implies that listening can go around and around up to four times, symbolizing four levels, the micro, meso, macro, and mundo, symbolic of the four development stages and worldviews and the four ways of organizing and structuring. With each round, our healing and creative learning can be experienced, interpreted, and integrated at deeper and deeper levels or paradoxically more expansively. Listening in this way is a very important creative activity, and a Servant-leadership capacity. Leaders need to listen to all stakeholders in the spiral, to the whole system, to all levels of the organization, or society. As we go around we find we have the capacity to attend to the four structures.

As we learn the disciplines and techniques of listening-first, our awareness and perspective on listening changes. Interiorly our skill capacity and awareness of our listening gains depth, breadth, and sensitivity. Exteriorly, our listening becomes more socio-centric, more globally expansive and inclusive. Growing our capacity for listening is mutually creative for our self and those with whom we listen, as our listening affirms and influences others. Holistic listening is inherently transformational, and choosing to listen for its transforming effect involves a quality of presence that allows us to intuitively and empathetically hear and discern what is emerging before us. The idea of being within a listening spiral can help facilitate our presencing and learning.

References

Data Filtering: QURA. (n.d.). Retrieved 2016 from https://www.quora.com/ Does-the-mind-record-everything-that-comes-through-our-five-physical-senses

Gandhi, M. (1913). From Vol 13, Ch 153, *General knowledge about health* (p. 241). Printed in the *Indian Opinion* on 9/8/1913 from *The Collected Works of M. K. Gandhi*, published by The Publications Division, New Delhi, India.

Greenleaf, R. K. (1977). *Servant leadership: A journey into the nature of legitimate power and greatness.* New York: Paulist Press.

Greenleaf, R. K. (1995). Reflections from experience. In L. C. Spears (Ed.), *Reflections on leadership: How Robert K. Greenleaf's theory of servant-leadership influenced today's top management thinkers* (pp. 22–36). New York: John Wiley & Sons.

Greenleaf, R. K. (1996). Types of leaders. In A. T. Fraker & L. C. Spears (Eds.), *Seeker and servant: Reflections on religious leadership* (pp. 89–100). San Francisco: Jossey-Bass.

Greenleaf, R. K. (1998). *The power of Servant Leadership.* San Francisco: Berrett-Koehler.

Greenleaf, R. K. (2003). In H. Beazley, J. Beggs, & L. C. Spears (Eds.), *The servant-leader within: A transformative path.* New York: Paulist Press.

Janusik, L., Fullenkamp, L., & Partese, L. (n.d.) *Listening facts.* Retrieved October 7, 2013, from http://d1025403.site.myhosting.com/files.listen.org/Facts.htm

McCraty, R. Bradly R. T., & Tomasino, D. (n.d.). *The heart has its own brain and consciousness.* Retrieved November 2016 from http://in5d.com/the-heart-has-its-own-brain-and-consciousness/

Morelli, M. D., & Morelli, E. A. (Eds.). (2002). *The Lonergan reader.* Toronto: University of Toronto Press.

Pearsall, P. (2007). In awe of the heart. Alternative therapies in health and medicine. *Research Library, 13*(4), 16.

Pennington, B. M. (2000). *True self false self: Unmasking the spirit within.* New York: Crossroads Publishing.

Sardello, R. (2008). *Silence: The mystery of wholeness.* Benson, NC: Golden Stone Press.

Scharmer, O., & Kaufer, K. (2013). *Leading from the emerging future: From ego-system to eco-system economies.* San Francisco: Barrett-Koehler.

Senge, P. M. (1995). Robert Greenleaf's legacy: A new foundation for twenty-first century institutions. In L. C. Spears (Ed.), *Reflections on leadership: How Robert K. Greenleaf's theory of servant-leadership influenced today's top management thinkers* (pp. 217–240). New York: John Wiley & Sons.

Sparough, J. M., Manney, J., & Hipskind, T. (2010). *What's your decision? How to make choices with confidence and clarity: An Ignatian approach to decision making.* Chicago, IL: Loyola Press.

6

Pathfinding-Foresight and Systems Thinking

On Foresight

Mankind has always been concerned with the future. We have always been interested in prophesizing about the future by predicting the weather, the stock markets, politics, what is happening to our city, our country, the future of humanity, and the evolution of the earth and beyond. Topics inherent to what is called futuring include an extensive continuum of activities that range from historical mystical prophesizing to the data-driven system models of the hard sciences. The purpose of futuring is to help us, personally and/or collectively, prepare, and adapt to what is arising before us.

Foresight and forecasting are differentiated categories within the topic of futuring; both categories are catch basins for multiple methods and models used to predict the future. Forecasting generally tends to include a variety of quantitative methods and applications for gathering historical and current data for interpretation and projecting futuristic trends, patterns, or possible scenarios. The general category of foresight tends to include less quantitative and more qualitative approaches to

© The Author(s) 2018
J. H. Horsman, *Servant-Leaders in Training*,
Palgrave Studies in Workplace Spirituality and Fulfillment,
https://doi.org/10.1007/978-3-319-92961-3_6

foreseeing future possibilities. Nonetheless, each category holds a mix of quantitative and qualitative methods, underscoring the value of integrating information from many ways of accessing and assessing data.

Our focus here is to explore and expand Greenleaf's notions on foresight, which fit best within the more generalized category of foresight. Greenleaf (1977) considered foresight to be the *central ethic of leadership* and *the greatest of the creative skills*, implying that foresight is so important that if it is not being practiced, leadership is not occurring. Greenleaf described foresight as a capacity of human consciousness. Developmentally, foresight is a state capacity functionally available to all, at all stages of human development. Given the primacy of foresight in Greenleaf's conceptualization of the Servant-leader, foresight is unquestionably an essential leadership capacity. To help differentiate Greenleaf's version of foresight from the general category of foresight and other foresight methodologies within the category, I have taken the liberty of renaming Greenleaf's version of foresight to *pathfinding-foresight*. What follows is a justification for this renaming along with elaborations on why pathfinding-foresight is the *central ethic of leadership* (Fig. 6.1).

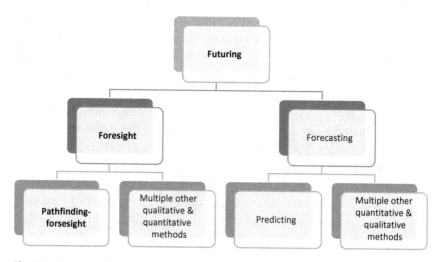

Fig. 6.1 Futuring, foresight, and forecasting. Printed with permission of Gonzaga University

Greenleaf on Foresight

Harold Leavitt (1987) in *Corporate Pathfinders* wrote that the great transformational leaders of history were and are pathfinders. Leavitt advocated that our educational institutions should place their primary focus on training pathfinders, rather than problem solvers. Pathfinders do not focus on figuring out the best way to get from here to there; nor do they focus on making sure that we get there; pathfinders seek the path we ought to go. Pathfinding is about drawing out and attending to the right questions, rather than getting right answers. The pathfinder is the "visionary, the dreamer, the innovator, the creator..." (p. 10). Pathfinding is about discovering and creating opportunities to enhance individual, team, organizational, community, and world flourishing.

Greenleaf's description of prophets, seekers, and leading, as three interdependent qualities of Servant-leadership, blends easily with the pathfinder.

> The *prophet* brings vision and penetrating insight. Within the context of a deeply felt and searching attitude the *seeker* brings openness, aggressive searching and good critical judgment. The *leader* adds the art of persuasion backed up by persistence, determination and the courage to venture and risk. (Greenleaf, 1996, p. 14)

Greenleaf proposed that all three qualities might occasionally exist in the same person, implying that more often the qualities are distributed within the leadership group or the general collective. Greenleaf's writing assumes an independent–interdependent role for foresight, emphasizing that both leaders and prophets must be seekers first. The seeker's role is to continuously search for the soundness, or rightness, of what is emerging by listening to prophetic voices (within and without), testing and seeking clarity of those voices, and, perhaps most importantly, discerning the timeliness of an emerging future. Servant-leadership is in part a pathfinder role.

Greenleaf (1977) indicated we are always experiencing two levels of consciousness; the first level is actively engaged in the world in a concerned, responsible, and effective value-oriented way. The second level is detached, riding above the first, viewing today's events, while being deeply involved in those events, with the perspective of a long sweep of history while projecting insightful implications into the indefinite future (pp. 25–26). Again, from the first level, we engage life acting and reacting based on our learned skills, values, and assumptions; from the second level (often less consciously), the adequacy of our values and assumptions is being examined with the aim of future revision and improvement (pp. 26–27). Greenleaf (1977) also stated that a qualification for leadership is that one can tolerate a sustained wide span of awareness so that one better *sees it as it is*, and in leadership positions, it is important to have the capacity to allow *creative insight* to function (p. 27). Greenleaf's description of the second level of consciousness is the creative foreseeing pathfinder capacity. The pathfinder role is to hold one's worldview loosely, always open to adaptation—like a relatively stable open system in perpetual transformation.

Greenleaf (1977) introduced greater complexity into his concept of foresight by linking foresight to the integrity of the leader and the leadership group. Integrity comprises our convictions out of which we are prepared to act morally and responsibly in the world. Taking this notion of integrity a step further, he stated: "…integrity is partly foresight, anticipating the conditions that must be dealt with and acting while there is freedom to act" (p. 207). He countersinks his point claiming that failing to use foresight and act is an "ethical failure" of leadership (p. 26). An implication for Servant-leaders in training is that pathfinding as the *central ethic of leadership* involves learning and discerning, and our integrity is related to foresight through our judgment and capacity for decisions where principles of conscience and a sense of urgency compel not just action but timely and strategic moral action toward what is perceived to be right and responsible. A second implication is that pathfinding-foresight is creative, holistic, and integrative in that it potentially draws on all that we know and potentially applies all of our capacities, values, and skills.

Pathfinding-Foresight

Pathfinding-foresight engages holistic listening, and similarly to holistic listening when we intentionally attend to pathfinding, we may become more aware of our creative pathfinding capacity (see Chap. 5: "Listening-

First"). As with learning holistic listening, Bernard Lonergan's proposed transcendental structure for *coming to know* provides an excellent contextual model (metaphor) for framing what occurs during the practice of pathfinding-foresight (Lonergan, in Morelli & Morelli, 2002). Pathfinding-foresight is operative within the transcendental principles *be attentive, be intelligent, be reasonable*, and *be responsible*. Building from Lonergan's principles, we will address the notion of *aware healing* and *creative learning* as an integral pathfinding dynamic in *coming to know*.

Metesi (2013) researched Greenleaf's writings and Lonergan's transcendentals and descriptions of *coming to know* and developed a model that helps structure pathfinding-foresight in a creative learning dynamic. Metesi conceptualized that vision emerges from a combined interaction of intellection, imagination, and insight:

> Intellection is the creative, cognitive capacity of a leader to strategically prepare, analyze, and anticipate (p. 3). …Imagination is the creative cognitive capacity of a leader to visualize scenarios, pictures, images, or symbols that complement or expand intellection (p. 4). …insight requires the intentional withdrawal, disorientation, and suspension (at least momentarily) of both intellection and imagination to attend to sensory impressions…and is concerned with a multi-directional widening and deepening of perception (pp. 5–6).

Assuming, intellection, imagination, and insight are involved in the manifestation of vision and are primarily but not exclusively operative in our sensory listening (be attentive) and intelligibility making (be intelligent) processes, as well as within our reasoning and judging (be reasonable) and our decisions and actions (be responsible) processes. Pathfinding-foresight, as with holistic listening, begins with intentionally attending to our sensing and intelligibility making, where drawing on all our knowledge and experience to interpret new sensory data, we apply *intellection, imagination*, and *insight*, to stimulate *creative learning* through vision formulation and conceptualization. Creative learning arises from our capacities of experience and knowing and intelligibility making. Creative learning, however, is only one part of the creative dynamic.

Lonergan added another potency to the vivacity of this *coming to know* model indicating that optimum learning includes both *healing love* and *creative learning* (Lonergan in Morelli & Morelli, 2002). Lonergan emphasized, to be creative we need insights, but "insights can only be implemented if people have open minds.... insights will not be grasped and implemented by biased minds" (p. 572). Lonergan lists four types of biases that limit and distort the creative learning process:

> The evasive bias of neurotic denial: the bias of the egoist whose interest is confined to the insights that would enable him to exploit each new situation to his personal advantage: the bias of group egoism blind to the fact that the group no longer fulfills its once useful function or mission: finally, the bias of those who blindly cherish the illusion that their knowing will get them through their social dilemma. (pp. 572–573)

Lonergan goes on to describe the nature and power *love* evokes as a transforming and *healing* effect on bias and hatred.

> Where hatred only sees evil, love reveals values. Love commands commitment and joyfully carries it out, no matter what the sacrifice involved. Where hatred reinforces bias, love dissolves it, whether it be the bias of unconscious motivation, the bias of individual or group egoism, or the bias of shortsighted common sense. Where hatred plods around in ever narrower destructive circles, love breaks the bonds of psychological and social determinisms with the conviction of faith and the power of hope. (p. 573)

Accepting Lonergan's notions of *healing love* as an active relational force that mitigates and transforms bias, and that it is a vital operative in coming *to know*, makes healing part of the learning dynamic. With regard to pathfinding-foresight, Lonergan's notions of the influence of healing love bring conscious love, or aware healing into the creative learning dynamic.

Figure 6.2 shows the *aware healing* and *creative learning* states as a coming to know spiral integration. Spiral integration depicts the healing and growth that may occur throughout the whole human system when growth or learning is experienced. Aware healing is depicted as the experience of opening the mind, the heart, and the will. Creative learning is shown as the dynamic operatives of insight, imagination, and intellection.

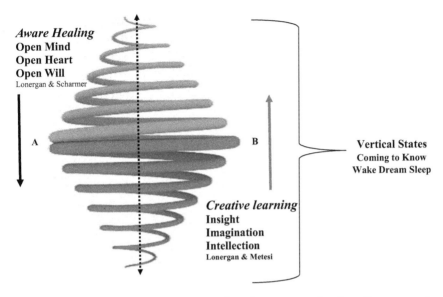

Fig. 6.2 Aware healing and creative learning. Aware healing (Lonergan & Scharmer) and creative learning (Lonergan & Metesi) symbolize an awake vertical state of coming to know that may occur in a moment of insight, or some other form of learning. Both spirals emerge in the present moment. The upper (lighter) spiral symbolizes aware healing descending from above and the lower (darker) spiral symbolizes creative learning arising from below. When both occur insights are less distorted and biased. Printed with permission of Gonzaga University (Color figure online)

Lonergan's insight is that the learning dynamic metaphorically involves two vertical developments (states experiences), one described as an *aware healing* movement from above radiating downward, while *creative learning* arises from below upward adding historical experience and knowledge to our experience with (Metesi's) intellection, imagination, and insight. The aware healing (love) dissolves or at least consciously suspends and abates biases, as in suspending the voice of judgment, the voice of cynicism, and the voice of fear (Scharmer, 2009). If one aspect of the dynamic should occur without the other, a distortion (limitation) arises in our perception and learning.

Aware healing and *creative learning* are two vital operatives of pathfinding-foresight. As with holistic listening, intentionally attending to the healing and creative learning process helps draw the creative process into our awareness. *Aware healing love* in this context becomes conscious and deliberate healing—at least in the effort of letting go. Lonergan's description of the debilitating effects of hatred and bias is quite similar to Scharmer and Kaufer's (2013) descriptive forms of *absencing* described as downloading, denying, de-sensing, deluding, aborting, and destroying (p. 24), all of which represent and perpetuate a progressive hardening resistance to healing and creative learning.

Scharmer and Kaufer's (2013) explanation of Theory U is an excellent methodology for experiencing, demonstrating, and learning pathfinding-foresight as both *aware healing* and *creative learning* can be experienced while journeying individually and collectively. Pathfinding-foresight is not only an individual capacity, it is inherently conducive to a collective capacity. When we engage pathfinding-foresight as a collective, I, You, We/It, and Source all become involved, and together we enact the *independent–interdependent* dynamic inherent to Servant-leadership. Opening the mind, the heart, and becoming willing and available, individually and collectively through co-presencing, co-sensing, and co-creating, opens us to empathetically practice generative listening and generative dialog to form collective conceptual iterations of an emerging vision.

As stated earlier, individually we all have access to the four stages of development all the time; however, where we reside at any particular time depends on the values and skills we are striving to learn and integrate. Practicing pathfinding-foresight is a way to learn from the future as it emerges before us. When we do a pathfinding U journey, we may transition back through the stages. In other words, if we are a Servant-leader in training at Stage III, the U journey may take us back through Stages I and II while building potential for Stage IV development. The journey back through the stages often involves healing and creative learning experienced as more holistic integration.

Pathfinding-foresight is a Servant-leader capacity that can generate hope and courage and provide direction when it is time to lead. The more clarity we have about our current reality, the greater is our potential for constructive pathfinding-foresight. The more present we are, or the less encumbered we are, by judgments, bias, inhibiting emotions, and fear, the more likely we are to foresee with greater clarity. We practice nurturing our pathfinding-foresight capacity so that it becomes available and helpful for developing an acute awareness of what is emerging at any moment. With awareness we can learn to consciously slide in and out of pathfinding-foresight as a way of practicing a more holistic integrated servant-consciousness.

Pathfinding-foresight is an aware healing and creative learning capacity to generatively glimpse patterns and images from the future to creatively envision and conceptualize new ideas and strategically and collaboratively evolve and integrate them into system frameworks.

Presencing

Presencing enhances our capacities for holistic listening and pathfinding-foresight. Presencing involves the combining of sensing and conscious presence (Scharmer & Kaufer, 2013). In addition to becoming more available in the present moment, presencing allows the juxtaposition of the historical past as well as the emerging future. Presencing enhances our capacity to access body wisdom through discerning, focusing, and gesturing, and it prepares us to access and be receptive to collective wisdom.

Presencing is a state conducive to healing (love) and creative learning (insight, imagination, and intellection). Presencing is a moment of true freedom, a moment when our knowing, our feelings, and our cautious will are in abeyance, and we are open and expectant—*present and available*—to sense the emerging future. A deeper interior aspect of presencing involves the subtle awareness and experience of ongoing inner presencing, a knowingly *being with* all that is occurring; this awareness is an aspect of the pathfinder capacity. Presencing is a state of transforming readiness, where we become open to transforming our notions of our identity and purpose. Shifts in awareness of our self and our future role may stimulate a greater sense of integrated wholeness and may enrich our worldview.

Presencing is also a collective activity. The *Four Breath Presencing Practice*, introduced in Chap. 7, is helpful for preparing a group for presencing. Applying pathfinding-foresight as a collective process may open a group to accessing collective wisdom. Collective wisdom may emerge from an individual (I), other group members (You), or the entire group

(We) and Source. From group presencing, a group may also experience a shift in identity, purpose, and clarify a more informed worldview from practicing pathfinding-foresight.

Systems may become blind to their own dysfunctions. A personal or systems blind spot is where we are stuck and do not know it. Discovering the blind spot often involves journeying to the frontier of our knowing, or to the margins of the system, personally or organizationally. Our stuckness has some recognizable features such as rigidity, resistance, and pain. Our stuckness manifests where we are unhealed, where the system is broke, where we are blind to our denial, where we resist with judgments, cynicism, and fear. We can notice stuck feelings in our body, and we can notice it in the resistance mirrored by members of the collective. Most of us know what it feels like when we are in a room full of resistance, and we can learn to attend to our own resistance, as well as that of others. Once discovered and acknowledged, our stuckness (resistance) actually becomes a gift as it becomes the threshold (doorway) to healing and creative learning and greater integrated wholeness.

Pathfinding-foresight is about perceiving (through presencing) what is emerging into our personal and collective system, discerning its relevance, and actively facilitating that emergence. Pathfinders look for, listen for, and learn to feel where the system is stuck or broken and empathetically seek awareness from that perspective. Willingly attending to our resistance dissolves (heals) threshold barriers and serves the greater integration of thought and feeling which in turn serve the development of a servant-consciousness.

The U Journey

Our pathfinding capacity is activated during the U journey (for more information see https://www.presencing.com/theoryu). Learning the creative processes inherent to pathfinding-foresight nurtures a foreseeing capacity while drawing that capacity into greater conscious awareness. The primary learning task for Servant-leaders in training is to draw their capacity for pathfinding-foresight into greater functional awareness, so that they might deliberately and consciously access this capacity at any moment in time.

Scharmer and Kaufer (2013) describe Theory U as a framework and a language for seeing and talking about our deeper levels of personal and collective experience. It is a methodology for shifting the place we come from as we work in the world and for operating from more holistic and integrative deeper levels (mind, heart, and will) more effectively. The U journey is a process for initiating and stimulating profound and progressive changes. The U journey evokes state experiences that may address first person, second person, and third person healing and creative learning.

The U journey is designed to be taken individually and collectively. The journey invokes pathfinding-foresight, especially when we are stuck and unable to move toward greater flourishing personally and/or collectively. The U journey is described and depicted as a descent to the bottom of the U followed by an ascent up the U. Whether descending or ascending, the journey passes through three distinct thresholds or zones. It is important for Servant-leaders in training to become familiar with and be able to recognize which zone they are in, as the state experience feels different in each zone. We can learn to recognize these zones by the relational feel and by what might occur in the different zones.

In descending the U, the first threshold, Open Mind, involves opening to learning by suspending judgment (bias) about what we know about the problem situation and opening ourselves to new information. Opening our mind entails opening to debate, with a focus of searching for information that will confirm our existing views; in this zone we remain grounded in a win/lose, right/wrong mentality. Suspending our judgments and directing our attention to the perspective of another is a way of opening the field of the mind to healing, by suspending bias, or at least reducing our resistance, so that new information might be heard. Open Mind is a familiar state of learning, as leaders we are comfortable in the cognitive realm where we learn through ideas, insight, and innovate ideas that might, for example, stimulate the redesign of systems and structures.

If our debating does not resolve the issue, we need to go deeper. In the more relational Open Heart state, our awareness is redirected from self to the field of others. In the open-hearted zone, our need for understanding draws us to attempt to understand the perspective of others; we empathetically strive to learn from their experience, insights, and dialog. These others may not have been listened to empathetically in the Open Mind state. When our heart is open, our cynicism is held in reserve, and we notice an inclusive connectedness to those in the group; this connectedness ranges from respect to compassion and love, and there is a greater feeling of trust and authenticity and a general sense of collective commitment and purpose. In the state of Open Heart, we find it much easier to practice forms of holistic listening. We find ourselves open to learning together and we are creatively open to supporting others and their ideas. The relational Open Heart is a natural and normal state for Servant-leaders. The relational empathetic state is where values and norms become the focus in attempts to reframe the issues in collective perspectives.

If our empathetic collective approach does not resolve the issue, individually or as a group, we may need to cross the third threshold into the Open Will, a state where we are present and available to what is arising from within ourselves, from other members, and from the group as a whole, as well as inspirations from Source. In this state we accept and hold our fear of the unknown in abeyance as we become open and available to what is emerging, and we creatively go with the flow. This is the bottom of the U, a space where identity and purpose can be re-created. When our will is open, we are in the moment (Kairos time), and we feel a sense of creative knowing; we may experience generative listening and generative dialog. We may be co-sensing and co-creating simultaneously. Healing and insights, images, and intellection are at work and whole thoughts may emerge and be taken up and passed around by others. The Open Will has a feel of trust as well as vulnerability; it is surrounded with meaning, generativity, and openness; and we feel alive with creative purpose. The leadership in the state of Open Will includes all who are present. Even though the healing and creative learning dynamic is active throughout the entire spiral journey, the dynamic is most transforming at the bottom of the U. While in a state of *letting go* and *letting come*, participants may access a field of possibility and inspiration, collectively participate in and experience co-presencing and co-creating. At the bottom of the U, we are most open to what Scharmer and Kaufer (2013) refer to as influence from *Source*.

Experientially, we can become aware of and learn to recognize the feel of the Open Mind, Open Heart, and Open Will as we descend the U. Ascending the U is described as a series of mini U journeys. So the sequential crossing of thresholds is not as clear, as we may ascend and descend through the three zones several times. Based on experience with these mini U journeys both in descending and ascending, I am convinced that the U journey is actually a *spiral state journey* (but the U is simpler to describe and understand).

At the bottom of the U, once an idea or an image emerges through the crack in our current reality, we grasp a hold of that idea or image, and we individually and collectively begin to work with it crystalizing, and conceptualizing and fashioning it into something usable. This begins the ascent up the U. As we ascend back into the Open Heart, we call on our relational helpers to provide input and feedback on our new creation, creating many iterations and learning from our ideas and models. We move further up the U when we begin making or practicing with prototypes. Prototyping involves creating multiple actualizations of the vision, failing fast, and often, as a way of learning until a viable solution is created and ready to be fitted into a functional performing system.

While ascending the right side of the U we are reminded to continue to be wary of bias, otherwise the creative healing process may become infused with, or distorted by, fear, cynicism, and old judgments. The capacity for ongoing presencing using pathfinding-foresight is integral to the entire experiential journey of the U spiral. Pathfinding-foresight is a healing and creative learning dynamic; it is optimally operative while *presencing* and accessing and working with personal and collective wisdom and is vital to developing greater capacity for systems thinking and strategy. Where we focus our attention creates potential for new awareness, thus by intentionally attending to a pathfinding-foresight process, we may enhance our capacity and expand our worldview.

Creativity and Pathfinding-Foresight

Greenleaf (1977) indicated, when we are alert, our awareness is open, we experience more intense contact with what is occurring around us, and we seem to have a greater access to information interiorly and exteriorly, and we may experience intuitive insights about what we are experiencing. We seem to be more engaged in a creative, holistic, and integrated way.

Even more to the point: "Except as we venture to create, we cannot project ourselves beyond ourselves to serve and lead" (Greenleaf, 1977, p. 257). If pathfinding-foresight is the *greatest of the creative skills*, how might we deliberately stimulate our creativity?

I often ask students the question: *Have you ever considered the importance of your own creativity, or your capacity for creativity?* In a typical graduate class, one or two students will indicate they may have taken a course related to creativity. Few students can recall the last time their creativity was affirmed. The vast majority of adult students have never intentionally attended to developing their creative capacity—inside or outside of academia. Nonetheless, with further probing and some reflection, students begin to recognize just how creative they actually are and how much they actually use creativity in their work and in their personal lives. As individuals and as groups, we have an innate capacity for creativity; we are pro-creative, re-creative, and co-creative; we are creative beings. Creativity may be what makes us most human: how might we enhance our awareness of our creativity?

Enhancing awareness involves working with our state capacities. As referred to earlier, state capacities are represented via different metaphors such as sleep, dream, and awake, or first person, second person, and third person. Our creative capacity both stimulates and flows out of these state experiences. Holistically, enhancing awareness in one state area may systemically influence the others. Becoming more aware (*awake*) seems to be the state experience with the most leverage for 2nd Tier development.

We know that wherever we place our attention that is where our energy, or the energy in the system, will go. "Energy follows attention" means that we need to shift our attention from what we are trying to avoid to what we want to bring into reality (Scharmer & Kaufer, 2013, p. 1). Suspending our judgments, redirecting our sensing, and quelling the voice of fear allow us to attend to sensing and intelligibility making. Interiorly we can learn to hold space and expand space for ourselves and others. When we intentionally attend to the practices of presencing, aware healing and creative learning, and generative listening and generative dialog, we may experience greater *spaciousness* interiorly and exteriorly. Learning to do this seems to enhance our awake state and may enhance our creative capacity, which in turn enhances our capacity for greater holistic integration.

Experientially, how can we stimulate this kind of spacious awareness? A three-stage creative change model (adapted from change management) can be described as shifting from A → *Not A!B* → B. State A is recognized as stable but no longer desirable (dysfunctional); getting to *Not A!B* involves destabilizing or creating a transforming state; B involves re-stabilizing a new (ideally more functional) configuration. The metaphor might represent an organizational, or systems, change process. The transforming state is *Not A!B* (the *!* between *A* and *B* signifies the crack through which inspiration emerges). Experientially *Not A!B* represents a transforming time and spatial shifts in function that may occur as slowly as melting ice bergs, or as fast a lightning. Some metaphors for the transforming state *Not A!B* might be *unknowing* or *the crucible* or a *desert experience*.

The first obstacle to overcome in the change process is resistance to change itself, the yearning to retain A, or resistance to the unknown *Not A!B*, or resistance to the new B. Some of the common feelings we have when we step into the unknown are expectancy, faith, fear, dread, perhaps terror, but also expectant hope. Once the change process begins, our resistance often creates a yearning (temptation) to regress and try to recapture a more comfortable and imagined simpler past (A), where discomfort supposedly did not exist; however, that just stalls or aborts the transforming process. When we become aware of resistance in any of these areas, we welcome it as a gift for it becomes the doorway to the solution. The solution is to fully step across the threshold into *Not A!B* and eventually emerge transformed at B. Letting go of our resistance opens up the possibility for movement and creativity.

What might be optimum conditions for *Not A!B*? A willingness to actually let go of A, with intentions of journeying to B, but with no clear conceptualization of B. Journeying while waiting for B to clarify involves letting go of the old (A), metaphorically dying to the old, freeing ourselves in a sense to be available to go with the flow. The reality is that the more we clutch onto A, the less likely B is to emerge much different than A. Also, while in *Not A!B* the more we yearn for a preconceived vision/idea of B, the less likely a true creative potentiality of B will occur. In other words, the more we are able to remain in the unknowing, willing to be present and available to not knowing, the more likely something truly creative might occur. The desire to control the change process is almost irresistible, but control limits the potentiality for the creation of B's uniqueness. This *Not A!B* state was similarly articulated by Scharmer (2009) as the state of *letting go* and *letting come* experienced at the bottom of U journey.

Creative change model A → *Not A!B* → B

Conditions for *Not A!B* (the creative pause)

- Let go of A with expectancy...faith...fear dread terror...hope...
- With intention and expectancy but no clear vision or experience of B...
- Attending to *Not A!B* while waiting, incubating, trusting, B will emerge
- When B emerges, act quickly to crystalize, conceptualize, and envision Bs potentiality.

When we reflect on a few of the major transforming experiences of our lives, we can easily identify with the vulnerability of being in *Not A!B* and may also become aware how important it is to not rush to B. Trust, faith, and process engender creativity. To enhance the transforming creative process, we need to learn to put our resistance aside (while remaining attentive and cautious) and accept the awkward uncomfortableness of *Not A!B*. This means first being aware enough to acknowledge where we are, and second practicing hanging out in the incubating, transforming cauldron. Importantly, we need to acknowledge that *Not A!B* is not a bliss or do nothing state, rather it is a very engaged state of being, a state of being *present and available* by suspending judgments and bias, overriding personal and cultural norms, and quelling the fear of the unknown. The experience of pausing in the dynamic state of *not knowing* (*Not A!B*), in my experience, enhances one's capacity to be with non-duality, increases comfortability with ambiguity and paradox, and stimulates insight and creativity, and that awareness benefits our personal growth as well as our organizational work.

The state of *Not A!B* challenges our issues with time. Hanging out in *Not A!B* involves allowing and honoring manifestations of both Kairos (momentaneity) and Chronos (sequential) time. In most change processes, we feel uncomfortable and vulnerable in *Not A!B*, and so we strive to get to B as quickly as possible. When we are manifesting *Not A!B*, we need to be most attentive to honoring Kairos while respecting Chronos; this means honoring the process and allowing ourselves to be in *Not A!B* knowing the incubation is necessary and trusting that we will know when it is time to move on. Actually, the more present we are to letting go and letting come, the more Kairos and Chronos seem to meld appropriately.

Not A!B symbolizes a creative transforming process and a state of creative potentiality. Knowing *Not A!B* is an *aware healing–creative learning* structure and process allows us to intentionally attend to it when we are there and acknowledge when we are not. To enrich the creative change process, we need to first have the wherewithal to realize when we are in *Not A!B*; this involves intentionally attending to the experience and the *feel* of the Open Will zone or field. Greater awareness of the healing and creative potential of *Not A!B* provides us a choice of what we need to do to stimulate the creative process when we find we are stuck. Once we have become familiar with the *feel* of the field, we can then learn to access it consciously. Once B emerges, we get to work; we grasp it and begin getting to know it, crystallizing and conceptualizing a clearer understanding of just what B is. Then the system thinking and the strategies for system change begin.

Practicing prolonging *Not A!B* for as long as the formative process takes builds creative capacity. Having the willingness to hang out in *Not A!B*, knowing A does not work for us anymore, while not wanting to force a premature arrival of B is, I believe, the emergence of a *transforming mind* (Kegan & Lahey, 2009) and a sign of emerging Stage IV development. More accurately, a transforming mind may include the capacity to know and lightly hold A, be in *Not A!B*, while also lightly holding a quasi-vision of B: this is consciously being in the *past*, the *present*, and the *future* at the same time—all the time. When we can live comfortably in knowing, and not-knowing, and in possibility, trusting that all is in motion, respond authentically to that motion, trusting that the motion is constructive and benevolent, and that a solution will emerge when time and space are ready is living in a creative flow. When creativity becomes part of our conscious disposition, we experience an internal sense of affirmation and wholeness, and insights and integrations appear to resolve, evolve, and flow with inspired gratitude and joy.

A creative capacity is necessary for each stage of our development. Imaginal skills are the kiln for creative, holistic integration, and each stage shift requires a greater capacity for conscious imaginative creativity. Beginning in Stage III, our awareness of our creative capacity and the ongoing fostering of our innate creativity needs to emerge into our conscious awareness in a deliberate and disciplined way. An even greater imaginal awakening along with a purposeful unleashing of creativity is the driver for Stage IV development. Acknowledging, affirming, and practicing creativity affirms our being, as we find meaning in and accept responsibility for revitalizing and even reshaping the environments in which we live. Creativity is part of the multifaceted disposition of the Servant-leader.

Stage IV development entails a capacity to adapt and change as we integrate, evolve, and create a more expansive and transforming cosmic worldview. At Stage IV a transforming mind coincides with evolving and transforming collectives (4.0 ecosystems, Scharmer & Kaufer, 2013). A transforming mind is not rigidly attached to what we think we know, or how we think things should be, or how things should be done, or even who we think we are. Embracing creativity at the higher stages involves a pliancy of mind and heart and the will to move with the resolving flow of what is emerging.

Vision Strategy and Systems Thinking

The capacities of the integrated strategist or Generative-servant emerge developmentally in Stage IIIB and Stage IV. As the world becomes increasingly more complex, the need for Servant-leaders with transforming capacities becomes increasingly more universal. Although there is a functional strategist capacity at each stage of development, the role takes on greater prominence and responsibility in 2nd Tier development as our worldview becomes more expansive interiorly and exteriorly and as we build capacity for a global systems framework in our minds.

Today, people tend to believe that strategic plans are not of much use because the world is changing so fast that plans become a constraint (a dinosaur) that restricts rather than encourages and enables innovation and adaptation. However, all the more reason to have a global systems framework (a Stage IV worldview) in our minds, so we can adapt and transform with the flow. The value of a strategic plan is that it structures, or to put it more flexibly it intends, our direction. The structure that intends the direction reflects the organization or societies core values. The core values guide the framework for achieving the direction. At Stage IV systems thinking is inherent to strategy and pathfinding-foresight.

Pathfinding-foresight is not only about creating a vision, it also involves discovering, creating, and influencing the ways to get that vision into the workings of the collective.

A futuristic vision is a flexible, adaptable, directional intention with structures and goals guided by clearly identified value priorities. The values, goals, and structures of the vision then become the guiding principles for a strategic framework and strategic set of initiatives. Even though we bring all of our current knowledge (data) and experience to the visioning process, pathfinding-foresight is the grounding work for building vision and strategy, as well as the primary capacity to go to when adaptive adjustment is warranted. Drawing on integrity and making timely responsible decisions and taking action calls forth timely leadership strategy. In a transforming collective, strategic plans will often need to be adapted, and even the system structures and the goals may need to be shifted and refined as time, new information, and events arise; however, the strategic plan holds the guiding values to return to for renewal and refocusing when systems become stuck.

Organizations that begin with vision embrace the potential to create a new future. Pathfinding-foresight is helpful for organizational redesign where new mental models and strategies focused on aligning core values with policies and organizing structures are sufficient to achieve the organizational vision. Pathfinding-foresight is also helpful when an organization engages a sincere reframing process open to reflectively examining a rearticulation and realignment of core values and beliefs in adaptive ways that help members re-conceptualize a more strategic vision and ways to achieve it. Pathfinding-foresight is most helpful when an organization needs to re-create itself with an entirely new vision (a paradigm shift) through generative creative visioning and learning from the emerging future. Becoming clear about our current core values and knowing when those core values have, or need to be, re-conceptualized is critical to shifting between worldviews. Clarifying the vision always comes before redesigning or re-creating strategy. Otherwise futuring without a vision is merely forecasting based on past history.

The more comprehensive the structure of a strategic plan, the more it will take into account and (potentially) be responsive to all parts of the system. Involving key stakeholders from the system gives them access to and a voice in the plan from the beginning. When all key stakeholder groups are represented in the strategic plan, the plan becomes adequately representative. More importantly the strategic plan can then be influenced by any individual or group of stakeholders when realignment with core values is necessary. An uninvolved key stakeholder becomes a voice crying in the wilderness, once a strategic plan has been created. Involvement helps keep everyone engaged and may reduce the natural tendency for leaders and their departments (striving for a sense of independence) to fragment within the system.

The purpose of organizational and system structures is to enable system efficiency. The strategic plan is a guiding frame of reference for organizational activity; if the structure restricts flourishing, it will need to be adapted. Importantly, the more organizational members are able to work with the systems perspective, the more they will be able to strategize and align their work with the organizational vision. Practicing pathfinding-foresight stimulates systems awareness and further develops our capacity for system thinking and strategizing.

A strategic plan can be concieved of as a relatively stable open system in dynamic transformation. The greater the system diversity, the more resilient the system once it has achieved a relative state of harmony. Empowering all people and groups in the system increases the responsibility of all participants to act when they see the plan is not serving them; this involves an independence–interdependence value awareness. Generative-servants focus on procedures and objectives and are able to easily slide in and out of a variety of roles and perspectives on multiple issues. The transforming skills of the Generative-servant enable them to reframe themselves and influence the reframing of groups, as well as organizations and communities, and even global systems.

Transforming skills invite empowering and collaborative solutions. Generative-servants draw on their awareness and experience of the *independence–interdependence* dynamic to help re-create themselves and their organizations by consciously and deliberately accessing pathfinding-foresight within themselves and others when things are stuck or deteriorating. This requires developing the internal capacity to holistically listen to and integrate multiple perspectives and learning to call forth and draw out collective wisdom. Rather than viewing ambiguities as problems to be stamped out, or ignored, as strategists Generative-servants creatively honor disparate points of view as gifts to help them integrate and use information to fulfill their leadership responsibility. The Generative-servant learns to accept and work with tensions and contradictions while searching for resolving solutions.

Pathfinding-foresight involves working the contradictions out of our worldview as much as possible. Contradictions show up as pathologies and incongruence. Practicing ongoing aware healing and creative learning helps us listen holistically, and to visualize, and conceptualize an actual system and how it functions or dysfunctions, so that we may discover where it is stuck and nurture movement toward greater systems harmony. Without a global systems framework, there is no way of knowing whether system adjustments are contributing to the problem, creating more problems, or if they are truly innovative with potential to produce greater flourishing.

In summation, aware healing and creative learning are core to pathfinding-foresight. Pathfinding-foresight is core for drawing forth individual and collective wisdom, for visioning and conceptualization, for creating and adapting strategy, for stimulating systems thinking, and for developing the capacity for a global systems framework, all of which contribute to a servant-consciousness. Awareness of our capacity for pathfinding-foresight involves being present and available to the future—all of the time.

Although integrative work occurs at each stage of human development, the integration of mind, heart, and will is most demanding at Stage IV development. It is demanding because the integration involves expanding our worldview and intentionally attending to drawing what was formerly unconscious into our consciousness. Such an integration is a huge developmental shift and a huge responsibility. Generative-servants thus become even more acutely aware and responsible for the application of Greenleaf's *best test*:

- *Do those served grow as persons?*
- *Do they, while being served, become healthier, wiser, freer, more autonomous, more likely themselves to become servants?*
- *And what is the effect on the least privileged in society; will they benefit or, at least, not be further deprived?* (Greenleaf, 1977, pp. 13–14)

References

Greenleaf, R. K. (1977). *Servant leadership: A journey into the nature of legitimate power and greatness*. New York: Paulist Press.

Greenleaf, R. K. (1996). Religious leaders as seekers and servants. In A. T. Fraker & L. C. Spears (Eds.), *Seeker and servant: Reflections on religious leadership* (pp. 9–48). San Francisco: Jossey-Bass Retrieved from https://www.presencing.com/theoryu

Kegan, R., & Lahey, L. L. (2009). *Immunity to change*. Boston, MA: Harvard Business Press.

Leavitt, H. J. (1987). *Corporate pathfinders*. New York: Penguin Books.

Metesi, L. (2013). *The significance of foresight in vision and narrative leadership*. Unpublished article, University of Wisconsin, U.S. Personal Communication.

Morelli, M. D., & Morelli, E. A. (Eds.). (2002). *The Lonergan reader*. Toronto: University of Toronto Press.

Scharmer, O. C. (2009). *Theory U: Leading from the future as it emerges*. San Francisco: Barrett-Koehler.

Scharmer, O., & Kaufer, K. (2013). *Leading from the emerging future*. San Francisco, CA: Berrett-Koehler.

7

Nurturing a Servant-Consciousness

Humility

Humility is a universal human value that may appear to be an unnatural element of leadership, yet we recognize that our wisest leaders and some of our most respected heroes exhibit this virtuous quality. Serving-first implies humility in acknowledging that we need others to become more whole. Humility grounds our being in our doing. Greenleaf's notion of *first among equals* implies humility within the notion that leadership is always plural. Humility runs through all stages of development and is recognized as a fruitful value in Beck and Cowan's 2nd Tier (Stages III and IV) of human development.

Writing about humility as it relates to Servant-leadership may sound prescriptive as the nature of humility can be awkward to convey. Humility does not reconcile with those who subscribe to *survival of the fittest*, or the reported heroic successes of many who practice *adversarial leadership*. Obviously, humility is not evident in *I win you lose* scenarios. Humility is challenging if we are personally struggling for acceptance and advancement. Demonstrations of pride and arrogance do not reflect humility and raise questions about our integrity. Integrity, humility, and the choice to

© The Author(s) 2018
J. H. Horsman, *Servant-Leaders in Training*,
Palgrave Studies in Workplace Spirituality and Fulfillment,
https://doi.org/10.1007/978-3-319-92961-3_7

serve-first reveal values that override the human desire to be a celebrity, to take from others, to keep from others, to advance at the expense of others, or to hold onto power or resources to the detriment of others (Anonymous, 2002).

For Servant-leaders in training, self-honesty is a critical test of humility. How we give and receive tests our humility. How do we receive gifts from those less powerful or those less affluent than ourselves? Are we truly gracious, or do thoughts of dismissal, embarrassment, arrogance, or justification run through our minds. Reflectively, a seemingly innocent desire to help (serve) can be a thin disguise for wanting to be the helper. Reflection on wanting to be the helper may expose all sorts of arrogant and prideful distortions, such as wanting to be seen and known as the helper, or wanting to paternalistically or manipulatively control and influence others. Humility is grounded in the realization that without the acknowledgment and commitment to something greater than ourselves, we are not likely to serve beyond ourselves.

As with many words, humility has evolved several connotations. For example, a common notion of humble implies *not worth much*, such as a humble home. Another common connotation is humiliation such as when a person, or a team, somehow humbles or humiliates another in a sport. Such meanings are not indicators of a profoundly relational disposition. Servant-leadership embraces a much deeper, richer, value-laden notion of humility.

The word humility was originally derived from the Latin word for humus (as was humorous), implying grounded and earthy with a rich fertile capacity. Some of the earliest Western writing on humility come from the Benedictines, the oldest order of Christian monks. The Benedictines pursue wholeness within a unitive relationship with God, with each other, with the human race, and with all creation. For the Benedictines this pursuit is a liberating experience that entails a commitment to stability, obedience, and continuous conversion (growth in awareness). These three commitments are viewed as foundational for the formation of humility.

The three vows of the Benedictines have echoes in Servant-leadership. A Servant-leader is profoundly relational; a monk's vow of stability implies a commitment to stay in relationship and in community. A monk's vow of obedience implies a commitment to learn to listen for the truth (the greater good) present in each situation; similarly a Servant-leader listens for clarity before influence and lives by moral principles in accordance with Greenleaf's best test. The Benedictine commitment to ongoing conversion experienced in the context of relationship and community nurtures a transforming mind, as well as compassion, generosity, gratitude, and joy. The Benedictine vows create grounding experiences for what they call the pursuit of a pure and humble heart—humility. Humility is more than an intellectual idea, it is way of being that is learned from reading, practice, experience, reflection on experience, feedback from others, and more practice. It requires a personal experiential life journey that engages interior work, serving others, and modeling Servant-leadership.

Humility is about being aware of and experiencing desires, and choosing to be free from, or at least indifferent to those desires. The distinction between desire and attachment is not readily understood or easily detached from. A natural desire can easily become an attachment, forming dependence that manifest as the need for things, the need for approval, recognition, security—the list can be long. Attachments tend to interfere with our capacity to function healthily and freely; they are an *add-on* (addiction) to a natural desire and sometimes that desire may become an obsessive must, something we grasp, cling, or grope for—or even die for. Purity of heart is about experiencing the desire without being compelled to act on it.

I am sure most can identify with the need to detach from a drug addiction, but that does not make the detaching easy. Treatment for addiction begins with acknowledging there is a problem and that we are helpless in our efforts to abstain. By acknowledging a craving and surrendering it to a *power greater than our self*, we may experience relief from the craving—if only temporarily. Practicing and learning to do this as a way of living begins a spiritual journey, a journey the monks have known about for centuries, a journey they refer to as *the twelve steps of humility*—a much earlier and somewhat different variation of what we commonly refer to as *The Twelve Steps* for getting relief from addictions.

The Benedictines understand the notion of attachment in a different context than our understanding of addictions; they identify the primary stumbling blocks to humility to be arrogance (pride) and insincere and inappropriate (false) humility, such as false modesty and doubt—both of which reflect interior and exterior dishonesty. It may seem easy to identify pride and insincerity as a problem in a destructive addiction; however, what about the good things we desire? What is wrong with being attached to good things? The fifth-century Christian monk John Cassian wrote that "anything which can trouble the purity and the peace of our heart must be avoided as something very dangerous; regardless of how useful and necessary it might actually seem to be" (Conference I.7, as cited in Kirkley).

The overall effect of being attached to anything distorts our perception and our freedom to be available. Attachments create distorted thoughts and feelings, feelings that become blurred by our wants, our cravings, and the fear of the loss of our attachments. These distortions create a filter that taints our lens of perception, altering our experience of events in the world; as a result, many events are misperceived and misinterpreted. Our distorting filters restrict our capacity to be *present and available*. Even a passion for Servant-leadership may detract from a healthy learning healing perspective when rigid understandings blur our clarity, and the result is a compromise of our transforming capacity.

Humility reflected in purity of heart requires further clarification. First, humility does not require one to not value one's own natural talents or gifts, or for that matter the gifts of others. We are not to dismiss or dishonor our gifts; not valuing or recognizing them would be disrespectful and dishonest. Second, humility does not mean one thinks less of his gifts than of similar gifts, or even inferior gifts, of others. We are not to compare and play down (degrade) our gifts and talents relative to those of others. Humility manifests when we value with profound respect the gifts of another which we may or may not possess (*Catholic Encyclopedia*). Humility is (in part) a capacity to accept and in a realistic sense be (humorously) amused by our limitations, while at the same time valuing and promoting those very aptitudes in others and, with this awareness having the courage to advance, or retreat, or remain silent.

We may be humbled then by the awareness of our attachments, by understanding the enormity of the struggle to be free of attachments, and by acknowledging one another's gifts. Awareness of the limitations of attachments and the struggle to be free of them is humbling, and even more humbling is knowing that we can only progress with Grace and the help of our community members. In serving others we reveal our gifts and our attachments; awareness of this is a humbling experience. When we are clear about this meaning of humility, we can understand why monks live in community; certainly, we cannot learn to be humble if independence is the greater priority.

For the Servant-leader, respect for the dignity of the human person is the crux of all relationships. Changes occur in our relationships when we can accept ourselves as we are and authentically and humbly love ourselves; this awareness arises from a sense of our true self—a self-more grounded and true than the ego self. Who we are, our presence, our integrity, our virtues, our faith, and our shadow and darkness communicate more than anything we can say in words—so this is what we must be attentive to in ourselves.

Humility begins with awareness and that requires rigorous self-honesty, as well as honesty from others. Once we become aware of an attachment, we then have a choice to pause and choose whether to allow the craving to run its course or, while acknowledging the desire, choose to surrender the inclination rather than be captured or controlled by it. When we do this, humility serves to cleanse our lens of perception and we experience enhanced awareness and freedom. Until we become aware of our attachment(s), good or bad, we do not truly have freedom of choice, and that lack of freedom distorts our availability and our sense of responsibility. Humility creates a capacity to be present and enriches the clarity of our purpose.

Another somewhat similar perspective on humility comes from the founder of another religious order. In the *Spiritual Exercises*, the Jesuit, Ignatius of Loyola, identified and described three modes of humility. For Ignatius, humility emerges from a focus on our relationship with God, but it can also be related to our spouse, vocation, organization, or community. For Ignatius, each mode is a variation in the quality of humility. The first mode of humility arises from a fundamental commitment to God (or our spouse, career, team), as in steadfast obedience to the relationship, such that betrayal, or severing the bond of the relationship, is not a consideration. The second mode of humility involves nurturing relationships through stability, realized as an expression of loving concern for the spouse, vocation, community, such that we live out our vocational commitment for better, for worse, for richer, for poorer, in sickness and in health, until death. This second mode involves consistency of one's commitment to the other in even the smallest ways, which involves an ongoing commitment to reduce self-centeredness and increase trust and service to the other. The third mode of humility involves an openness to continuous conversion of the heart, moments of honesty, and self-revelation that only the heart can know and understand. This is when we desire and willingly prefer to share the depths of the suffering and hardship, the poverty, and rejection of others, such that ultimately one would willingly die for the other—the ultimate act of humility. Humility is a quality of being that increases with our commitment to relationship (Sparough, Manney, & Hipskind, 2010).

Humility, it seems, is rooted in, and arises from, the depths of interior silence. Though we make efforts to clear away what may be inhibiting our capacity to be present and available, we do not go around speaking of the benefits of humility, except perhaps, for the purpose of teaching. A humble person feels no inner urging to speak of humility, and doing so feels like a violation of humility. In this sense humility is paradoxical, as humility always appears to be both apparent and hidden. We do not hide our humility, we live it outwardly, but the essence of its being remains veiled. "Others may see us as calm, collected, and serene, and wonder about where our serenity comes from and how we got that way" (Sardello, 2008, p. 93); however, all they see of humility is the fruit. Humility is a non-intrusive way of being.

Committing to becoming a Servant-leader in training calls forth the transforming qualities of humility. Humility involves realistically accepting that we have talents, limits, and inabilities based on an honest self-awareness of our strengths and potential. In this sense, humility is an antidote to ego inflation. Humility provides us with the awareness and will to search for pride and arrogance within ourselves. Until we accept ourselves as we are, we can make little progress on humility. Practicing humility involves serving-first and striving toward greater socio-centricity.

The natural desire to *serve-first* implies humility and empathy helps nurture humility. We often come to know humility by witnessing and experiencing it being modeled by others. Also, like Servant-leadership, we do not really learn to develop and value humility until we try it on in practice. Humility is self-revealing. Our humility, or lack thereof, may become very evident when we promote others over ourselves—a test of humility. A healthy focus on the responsibilities involved in calling forth others (and organizations) requires some humility.

The yearning to serve points to an awareness that greater meaning and wholeness can only be realized through other-oriented serving, not self-serving. Developing a profoundly relational capacity involves greater ego transparency, evidenced as humility and a clearer orientation toward meaningful relationships. As our capacity to value others becomes more expansive in Stage IV, humility becomes the primary grounding principle for Servant-leadership—a principle that embodies a spirit of compassion, generosity, gratitude, and joy.

Holism and Wisdom

Within the understanding of human development is the assumption that human progress advances with the clarification and expansion of knowing. Much of Greenleaf's writing is wisdom literature. As an elder, Greenleaf was passing on what he had learned from experience, information, knowledge, and wisdom. Accessing wisdom is part of the pathfinder role for Servant-leaders in training. The philosophy of Servant-leadership adheres to some assumptions about wisdom. Most importantly, individuals have access to wisdom and groups have access to wisdom, wisdom is always available in every situation. A Servant-leader may learn the discerning (sifting and distilling) wisdom skills of a wise elder. The work of the elder is to seek clarity without bias (attachment). The Servant-leader seeks to draw wisdom from knowledge and information, from attending to interior and exterior relationships, from sensing, and from spiritual experiences. Servant-leaders strive to develop the capacity to readily access, experience, discern, and use wisdom for relational functioning and in the structuring of organizational and collective systems.

Since the last renaissance we have relied more and more on scientific knowledge to guide our efforts toward human flourishing, today, however, it seems humans are being influenced more and more by mere information that relentlessly arises from the global network systems. Unfiltered fragmented information blows here and there, generating much wind and some devastating storms, producing questionable progress, threatening global regressions. The proliferation of information is a great challenge and a great opportunity. A great task for Servant-leaders in training is to awaken and revitalize the role of the wise elder in each of us. Globally a large portion of humanity is poised for a shift into 2nd Tier development. Never in the history of humanity has there been as great an opportunity to create such a large global shift. Today, the world is in need of many wise elders.

Our forefathers and foremothers relied on the sifted and distilled wisdom of the ages to sustain, promote, and create human progress, human flourishing, and cultural perpetuity. Even though our forefathers bequeathed to us an abundance of guiding wisdom in literature and the arts, for many today, wisdom has become less visible amidst the prolific generation of information arising from technological fragmentation and the immediacy of the moment. We seem to have forgotten where and how to search for wisdom within ourselves, and collectively. At best, we treat wisdom like factual knowledge because that is what we have learned is most important. Wisdom interpreted as factual or rational knowledge seems vague, or awkward, and, like myth, is often viewed as interesting but not really relevant.

Wisdom, however, is more than information or rational knowledge, it is another way of knowing and coming to know; wisdom is transrational. Wisdom is information and knowledge—plus; one might say it is inspired knowledge, or knowledge with vitality—knowledge vital to life flourishing. Wisdom is ancient, current, and ahead of its time. Wisdom is available to all and is always available. Wisdom offers a glimpse of a greater whole, it offers insight, plus it holds a foretaste of generative potential.

At times, during meditation, or solo walks, or from just being in Nature, we may hear wisdom speaking to us, through flowers or a cactus, or birds and animals, or the trees, or from water, or air, or stars, or even the earth itself. We can even learn to listen to wisdom speaking through silence. As mentioned, wisdom also speaks through individuals, and groups, offering healing and teaching for the benefit of the collective. Whatever the Source of wisdom, it seems that it speaks, and can be heard, through all of creation. Wisdom is holistic, evident in its ways of becoming known.

When we reawaken (bring into consciousness) our capacity to listen to wisdom, however it may speak, it is like something comes alongside our inner presencing, we recognize this knowing, and we intuitively sense we are hearing and witnessing something important, and somehow our knowing of this is being affirmed. When we attend (holistically listen) to wisdom, we get more than just cognitive information, wisdom is always somewhat relevant, and it ignites healing and creative energy that nurtures relational vitality. Also, the wisdom that emerges is sustained by greater wisdom, as the more we ponder wisdom, the more insight and clarity emerges. Wisdom not only emerges spiritually from within ourselves, it emerges through our body sensory system, through our insightful intelligibility making, through our relational heart knowing, and through our cognitive knowing. And it emerges similarly from other individuals and may be recognized and interpreted by different members of a group. Wisdom may be both specific and general, as well as inspirational to an individual and a whole group, in multiple ways.

Developing wisdom capacity involves learning to consciously access wisdom holistically. Wisdom is accessed holistically when we are present and available, when at least one other is involved, when we engage heal and create as a collective, when we are present to sacred space and Nature, and when we are open to inspiration from God, the Source of all that is and is not. When wisdom is accessed holistically, clarity comes easier, understanding is less distorted, and coming to know is more complete. Learning to deliberately access personal and collective wisdom is a listening and a pathfinding skill capacity for Servant-leaders in training.

Humanity has always had ways of accessing wisdom, and there is an age-old holistic structure for accessing wisdom. The structure is I, You, We/It, and God/Source/Spirit. Wisdom speaks through I; through You; through the collective We and It (the collective group, culture, and systems) and through Nature and the Great Benevolent Creative Mystery—or whatever name you prefer to use. The four-part structure is inherently a wisdom structure due to the inherent inclusivity and is sacred in the sense that it is likely as ancient as human consciousness. The spiritual enlightenment of mind, heart, body, and being (Delman, 2018) addressed in Servant-leader development (Chap. 3) appear to be embedded in the wisdom structure and may be the impetus for a profoundly relational, creative, holistic, and integrative disposition, and the evolving of a servant-consciousness.

Wisdom is always available in space and time. Accessing wisdom is always sacred work, and accordingly the work entails paying attention to the sacred, in ritualistic ways. The result is, processes seem to be more responsive when space and time are acknowledged as sacred. The spatial structures for creating a forum conducive to accessing collective wisdom are of great importance. There are many sacred spaces in our environment; they can be found in nature, in some of our building (sanctuaries), in our homes, and even in our hearts. These sacred spaces work best when nature and the beauty around us are gratuitously invited in. Beauty clarifies the invisible in the visible. When we invite in the beauty that is around us, we are respectfully opening to sacred spaciousness within our awareness.

The notion of spaciousness is important; it is a respectful, expansive receptivity to what is available and emerging. Interiorly we create spaciousness when we open our minds, our hearts, and our wills. Exteriorly we create spaciousness when we welcome whoever shows up, as an individual, as members of groups, as well as the mutually created persona of a whole group, and Source. This respectful empathetic heartful caring and inclusion inspires yearnings for human good. When we are in sacred space doing sacred work, both Chronos and Kairos time seem to harmonize; we often become aware of this after the fact.

Nurturing collective wisdom begins with stimulating the creative imagination within ourselves and within others. Holistic engagement involves holding our view of reality (our worldview) lightly so as to access the pathfinder. It also involves being warmhearted toward relationships. It involves attending to our sensory and intelligibility making processes. We may access all of these through multiple methods, such as discernment, through love, through gestures and a variety of other focusing techniques, through the steps of humility, and through the U methodology.

Generative-servants use holistic and integrative discerning processes (methodologies) that engage *I, You, We/It,* and *Source*; this four-part wisdom structure lends itself to innumerable potential approaches for accessing wisdom (this structure does not insure wisdom will arise, but committed engagement with the structure can be potent). *The Four Breath Presencing Practice* and the *U* journey are examples of methodologies or practices we can use to stimulate availability and greater clarity. For the Generative-servant, decisions always emerge from a We/It perspective, even when acting autonomously. Seeking collective wisdom is not about seeking compromise, it is not even about unanimous agreement. It is more about seeking and valuing the harmony amidst a diversity of perspectives. Seeking harmony may involve some influential persuasion, but it is more about conceptualizing the clarity of our listening and our collective knowing. Wisdom can be found in the harmony; the greater the harmony in the diversity the greater the clarified wisdom. Generative-servants strive to align with the creative life forces that make ecological balance possible (Hall, 1994). Transcendent truths may then become expressed, for example, by creatively using technology to work within the natural flow of the earth's ecosystems.

Figure 7.1 depicts the interdependent relationship of the hero and the elder. State experiences occur in the present moment: aware healing descends; creative learning arises. Not A!B is a transforming moment. Slowing the Not A!B process creates more space for insight, intuition, inspiration. Letting go and letting come occur on the *threshold of presence*. The nadir and the zenith are related and yet distinct aspects of a state experience—one that embraces humility at the nadir *Not A!B*, the other agape love at the zenith *Not A!B*. The hero's journey is a descent from A to *Not A!B* (humility) and an ascent to B, whereas the elder's journey is to continue the ascent from B to *Not A!B* (love) and a descent to a new more expansive revitalized A. For both hero and the elder the descent involves aware healing and the ascent involves creative learning. A metaphorical image for the hero and the elder is one of breathing out and breathing in. The hero exhales descending from A pauses at the nadir *Not A!B* and then begins to inhale again ascending to B. The elder continues inhaling from B to the zenith *Not A!B* pauses, then exhales on the descent to a revitalized A. The potential for aware healing and creative learning (holistic transformation) occurs in the space ! state of the pause. The interrelationship is that the deeper the hero goes into humility the greater the elder's expression (capacity) for love.

Waking Up the Wise Elder

Many of the most renowned mythological and historical wisdom teachers and leaders have been elders (regardless of their actual age). The very nature of leadership involves the future; we attempt to figure out where to go and lead into the unknown. When we are experiencing a leadership crisis, or struggling with how to lead, it may be helpful to study leaders in mythology. Mythology conveys wisdom. Mythology serves us when we need to foresee.

Similarly to dreams, mythology arises from state experiences, revealing insights and truths. Mythology is not grounded in scientific or historical fact; nonetheless, mythology does speak to us at cognitive, emotional, physical, and spiritual levels, at times when we are listening. Listening to mythology, being present and available, may occur holistically, or in part literally, metaphorically, allegorically, or analogically (spiritually). Mythology conveys rituals, signs, symbols, images, and characters helpful for interpreting where we have been, where we are now, and our journey forward. Mythology provides clues to what to attend to in our natural rhythms and our deep knowing, in our society, and in the natural world. Mythology as story may provide hope (an aspect of wisdom) when our systems are stuck, when we have no relevant data, and when past knowledge is not solving our current problems.

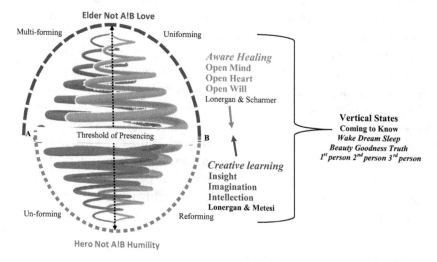

Fig. 7.1 The hero and elder's journey. Aware healing (Lonergan and Scharmer) and creative learning (Lonergan and Metesi) relate vertical state coming to know experiences that occur in the present moment (awake, dreaming, or sleeping). The red spirals depict the hero's self-learning for the collective (descent) and blue relates to the elder's learning relational values and skills in the collective (ascent). Both the hero and the elder are necessary for mature development. Printed with permission of Gonzaga University (Color figure online)

The *Journey of the Elder* related here is a stretch beyond the classical hero and portraits the role of the Servant-leader and the Generative-servant. To depict the *Hero and Elder's Journey*, I have adapted Joseph Campbell's (1986) descriptions of the *Hero's Journey*. Campbell studied mythology from many different cultures. Near the end of his career, Campbell concluded that our mythology was lacking something. Campbell emphasized that globally we are in need of a universal human myth for our particular time in history. After many years of musing, it has become clear to me that the *Hero's Journey* depicts only half of the mythic journey. The *Hero's Journey* offers much to the Servant-leader in training at the personal level where we struggle for autonomy and independence, but does not offer much for leadership of the interdependent collective. What is missing is a clearer depiction of the *Elder's Journey*. The elder's journey balances and grounds the hero's journey and is in part a mirror of the hero's journey being played out in the collective, with some distinct differences.

Developmentally the hero emerges most prominently in the 1st Tier of our development. The hero archetype addresses the struggle of individual and social pathology and the need for healthy healing, acceptance, recognition, and the restoration of independence. Historically our Western tradition has viewed the hero as the primary go-to archetype to lead and address our societal problems; today, however, our hero archetype seems to be stuck, perhaps because the hero's journey is mostly about the hero.

Wise elders abound in mythology, though they normally take a more humble, supportive, teaching, mentoring role to the hero. Actually, in mythology, it is the elders who call forth, guide, encourage, and nurture the hero. The elder archetype in mythology is much less emphasized, less celebrated, even though the elder is often wiser, more influential, and more relationally inclusive than the hero. The elder reflects 2nd Tier priorities.

The archetype of the wise elder evolves from the hero. Heroes focus on getting their life together, integrating and embellishing their gifts, and saving society, then returning to their pursuit of independence. However, if the hero's gifts are not transformed and fully gifted to the collective, the hero loses momentum and becomes self-obsessed—stuck. Perhaps the hero's journey was all that was necessary for 1st Tier societies, as the hero speaks directly to the yearning for independence and recognition. Today, however, with the complexity of our systems, the size and nature of our global organizations, and the diverse global challenges before us, we need a mythology that speaks to the macro and mundo struggles of 2nd Tier development. Wise elders not only give away their life, they more importantly give away their death, offering their wisdom, a gift that is most meaningful for the long-term perpetuity of the global collective.

The hero's journey involves personally seeking greater light in terms of awareness values and skills, sharing them and often setting a group or a community on the right path again; however, it often seems to be a temporary fix. The elder's journey, however, is more long term and involves the whole system; the journey entails preparing the gift to lighten our collective darkness—to nurture collective perpetuity. The collective darkness is our social pathology; it is where our culture, our systems, and our collective worldviews are stuck.

Like the personal and the relational (A and B) aspects of our human nature, the hero and the elder are a duo and each mirrors the other in some respects. The hero and the elder may or may not be the same person; both have tasks that arise from a need for transformation—the former primarily at the interior personal level, the latter primarily at the exterior collective level. The purpose of the hero's and elder's duo journeys is to bring greater flourishing to both individuals and the collective.

The hero undergoes and experiences a mystical journey and is gifted with healing insight and is transformed in some way, whereas the elder intuits and imparts new knowledge and new wisdom as a teacher, and heals and transforms the collective system. The hero's journey happens guided by greater and wiser forces, whereas the elder undertakes the responsibility for the journey and knowingly and visibly works with the forces that are available to guide transformation.

The Hero's Journey

The hero's journey begins with a departure from A (Fig. 7.1), crossing into the *threshold of presence* and descends to *Not A!B* to eventually emerge at B with a personal insight or healing gift. The hero's journey is primarily interior involving getting our life together and giving our life away to the collective, to resolve some personal or related system issue. The hero's primary purpose is personal transformation, to heal incongruence within our self and bring that awareness and healing into our life and then use it to serve the collective. In the descent from A, the hero experiences resistance and receives assistance from guides or helpers (elders); however, arriving at *Not A!B* is a solo and humbling experience. At *Not A!B* the hero receives a teaching, a transforming gift. On the ascent to B, the hero again meets similar or different guides (usually elders), experiencing resistance and help along the way. The journey is about conversion, having our baggage stripped away (*unforming*) and purification (*reforming*). The hero's journey always seems to involve a struggle with letting go of our former worldview and embracing our future calling (vocation).

On the ascent to B, the ongoing reforming prepares the hero for a clearer perception of the gift at B. The gift is specifically designed for the hero, providing the hero is willing and available to receive the wisdom. To the extent the hero is not fully available, the gift is distorted, interpreted as stolen, or interpreted in light of the past rather than the present and a brighter future possibility. The journey to B is about getting our self out of the hole we have created and become more whole. Emergence at B is a renewal; it may feel like a resurrection, accompanied by new insight, energy, and perspective. Often, there is a struggle at the threshold before B, as the hero meets resistance, or resists leaving the sacred journey. Heroes intuitively know they cannot return to the way it used to be. The catch is that the gift offered to the hero is not only for the individual's wellness, it is also for the well-being of the collective, usually family, or a small group, sometimes a macro society. The hero's journey is primarily a micro–meso journey. Unless the gift is generalized and passed on to the collective, and taken up by an elder, the gift may lose its transforming power.

The Elder's Journey

The purpose of the elder's journey is to change the world. The elder's journey is a reverse crossing; it is primarily about actualizing community for the purpose of ensuring collective perpetuity. The journey is about honoring, affirming, and demonstrating collective interdependence. The journey involves taking the personal gift B and transforming it in such a way that it can be used to expand and revitalize **A** within the collective—shifting **A** to a more expansive inclusive location on the spatial spiral (Fig. 7.1).

On the ascent to *Not A!B*, the elder's task is to include others, to teach them about the gift, so that it may be passed to a knowledgeable and accepting collective. The journey from B to *Not A!B* at the zenith is always about service, further purification (of self and others), giving our life away in service to family, organizations, and others in the collective. On the journey from B to *Not A!B*, the elder continues what began as the hero's transformation of self and works to transform the hero's gift into a more collective culturally acceptable enduring gift. In the transformational process, the elder gives his life away serving the greater good. In this sense it is about creating a congruent mirroring of the interior with the exterior, for the benefit of the collective. The elder's journey is about the transformation of people, institutions, and society, primarily at the meso, macro, and mundo levels, but there is an ongoing micro (personal transforming) also.

The elder's journey is an uphill struggle; it is about refining what is most meaningful about the gift, transforming it into an artifact that will serve the collective system (*uniforming*). The elder's struggle is to influence and persuade, heal, teach, and illuminate a new world (systems) view. The elder's responsibility at *Not A!B* is to die to the gift, to lovingly and freely give it away to the collective. The elder understands the risk of the endeavor. The risk is that those in the collective who receive the gift may ignore it, or due to their desire to be great take the gift and hold it from others, or use it to advance at the expense of others. At *Not A!B* the gift no longer belongs to the hero or the elder, it belongs to the collective. The gift has been transformed into an artifact of some kind (a work of art, a system, a new idea) and if it is worthy becomes generative for those who grasp its essence—and perhaps for those who do not. The challenge for the elder at *Not A!B* is to offer the gift—and let go. The gift is for the calling forth of others, who choose to take up its purpose and meaning and continue the journey.

On the journey from the zenith *Not A!B* to revitalized *A*, the elder becomes more and more invisible, for the journey is no longer about the elder, the elder no longer controls or guides the gift. Elders disappear (transform) as we give our actual or symbolic death away: like Leo in *Journey to the East* (Hesse), or Gandalf in *Lord of the Rings* (Tolstoy). Giving our death away is symbolic of illumination, giving away wisdom;

it is no longer even a legacy from the elder's perspective. However, from time to time, at **A**, the elder may symbolically, or magically, re-appear to affirm and acknowledge and sometimes clarify the gift; and, if necessary, generatively revitalize the meaning of the gift.

Distinctions

In myth, once the threshold A has been crossed, the hero's descent to *Not A!B* and the ascent to B tends to just happen. The hero seems to get caught up in a flow of spiritual energy and events. Up to this point in human history, learning leadership for most people seemed to just happen along with one's career; or at best, it was learning leadership primarily from parents, teachers, and mentors. Some people tend to be natural leaders; many others have to learn leadership through training and the school of experience. Where the hero's journey, for the most part, seems to happen to us, the elder's journey arises as a moral responsibility, a deliberate choice, an act of selfless love arising from the hero's journey. In a sense the elder realizes the responsibility of the gift and is compelled to offer it. The elder's journey is more visible and deliberate and requires persistence, training, creativity, and strategizing. Interiorly, the elder practices spiritual disciplines to develop a transforming mind, heart, body, and being.

The elder's journey is about serving-first. The elder's ascent from B to *Not A!B* and the arrival at revitalized *A* is a Servant-leader's journey, an exterior journey about bringing the gift to the collective. If the elder has not done the interior work, he/she will become frustrated, angry, cynical, and likely experience burnout. The journey from B to *Not A!B* involves developing the capacity to absorb, learn, and give away the gift, and that requires the strategic use of skills, vision refinement and re-conceptualization, and interdependent collaboration with many others; this involves the integration of humility and love.

In the ascent the elder develops a global systems perspective drawn from and informed by people, places, and things encountered along the way. The elder learns to compassionately expect system struggles, and the journey includes gathering support and working interdependently with others and within current systems. The elder's focus is on influential persuasion. The elder does not view the struggle from B to *Not A!B* as a battle against a dysfunctional system. The elder compassionately understands from a global systems view and out of generosity just keep showing up with the gift. If the gift is pure, it will eventually be perceived; that, however, does not mean it would not also be resisted or misconstrued.

Revitalizing *A* requires a hero and an elder's (I, You, We/It, and Source) journey. The elder models and guides the way. To model the way, the elder reflects on all that the hero has learned and draws from others to improve the human systems. The elder experiences and further refines the hero's transformation as we struggle to complete our sacred task. In doing so, the elder more fully integrates the hero's journey illuminating the gift to a more visible universal value for the greater society.

Servant-leaders in training may represent the hero or the elder, or both. Sometimes, the elder calls forth the hero, and sometimes the hero calls forth the elder. Sometimes it may seem the hero and the elder are traveling together calling each other forth simultaneously. Sometimes it is clear who the elder is and who the hero is, even though they may be very different people; the role, however, can change as it oscillates back and forth between them. As a result, the collective groups, organizations, or communities may all journey along with the hero and the elder.

An intrinsic truth within myth is that most humans experience and know this mythological journey consciously or unconsciously; more importantly, we each have a gift (perhaps many gifts). Inherent within the gift is the potent wisdom for nurturing individual and collective flourishing. In our time, there has been much attention placed on the hero, such that the gift is often clutched too tightly at the expense of the greater society. As I have stated, our global society needs many wise elders. Greenleaf emphasized, we need to begin preparing ourselves for our elder-hood today.

Anyone and everyone has the capacity to be an elder, at any time. Greenleaf indicated our destiny (as Servant-leaders in training) is to become wise and caring elders—Generative-servants. The wise elder seeks clarity, truth, and wise insight and a capacity to gift it all for the long-term flourishing of the collective. In learning to embrace, accept, and more consistently use the notion of serving-first, we can imagine, especially in challenging situations, that our role is that of a wise elder. In any given situation, what can we do differently in the role of a wise elder? How might the awareness *I am a wise elder, among wise elders* change our perspective and our judgments and our decisions? The wise elder's approach is profoundly relational, creative, holistic, and integrative.

Four Breath Presencing Practice

Developing a servant-consciousness involves expanding, affirming, and nurturing our awareness of our relational interdependence. When we bring relational awareness into our breathing through habitual practice using creative imagination, we may stimulate greater relational awareness and nurture a greater relational capacity. *Four Breath Presencing Practice* focuses on the way we breathe as a way to stimulate greater *I–You–We/It* and Source awareness. The practice creates spatial awareness for our relationships and augments our sense of relational responsibility. The *Practice* is designed to stimulate our imagining capacity and nurtures a greater integrative awareness of spirit, mind, heart, and body and may prove helpful for growing our capacity for a profoundly relational, creative, integrative holism.

The framework of *Four Breath Presencing Practice* is a rhythmic cycle of four successive breaths. A complete four breath cycle begins with a prayer for the well-being of our oneness and inclusively progresses to those we love, to all our known relationships, and finally to our relationship with all that is. With each successive breath we consciously attend to more relationships, such that each breath is intentionally more inclusive and exponentially more relationally expansive. In other words, the rhythmic cycle proceeds from the micro (self) expands to the meso (familial group), then to the macro (all whom we know and interact with), and finally to the mundo (all living things, the entire earth, and beyond).

The practice is inherently organic and is helpful for grounding and centering. A complete cycle takes 60–90 seconds (or longer depending on the detail we might choose to include). The cycle may be repeated as often as we feel inclined, anytime we feel inclined. It is most helpful to make the practice a habitual daily routine, done at the same time in the same (sacred) place, with stillness and quiet. The *Practice* can be done sitting, kneeling, and standing, walking, or running. (The practice can be done lying down, but this is not recommended as it further confuses our vertical and horizontal awareness.) The *Practice* is most impactful in stillness and quiet.

Intentional and attentional awareness for this practice is somewhat complex and involves a workout for our imagining capacity. The practice initiates a multidimensional creative activity that functions in the foreground of our mind as we imagine, observe, and track each breath. Each breath involves imagining, inhaling, and exhaling in seven directions. To begin, pause briefly to prepare, then visually and imaginatively inhale vertically from the earth (up through your feet) and from the sky (down through the top of your head) into the interior heart and corpus area, while simultaneously inhaling horizontally consciously and visually from before you, behind you, from each side of you, into the interior of the heart (the infinite interiority is the 7th direction); pause and then exhale physically while imagining exhaling spatially from the interior of the heart in all directions simultaneously. Doing this creates awareness of being grounded and centered and a greater sense of spatial awareness and connectedness with those around us.

The brief pause before inhaling and exhaling is a *transforming pause*, a preparation for what is going to happen next. The pause before inhaling prepares us to receive interiorly what we are in most need of. The pause before exhaling prepares us to offer what is truly most needed for ourselves and our relations. With each breath we inhale all the Blessing and Grace we are all in most need of (let God, Source, choose the nature of the Blessings and Grace); pause and then exhale healing love in all directions, to all intended within that breath. Note that the exact wording of the practice is not as important as the intention of the action. Again, after the first breath, each succeeding breath includes all the intensions of the previous breath, making each successive breath sequentially and exponentially more expansive and inclusive.

The central design of the *Practice* is the ongoing stimulation of the imagining skills deemed integral for expanding relational awareness and creative capacity development. In addition, the *Practice* is helpful preparation for all, or any of, four interrelated purposes:

1. Preparing for whatever we are to do next,
2. Preparing for presencing,
3. Preparing for accessing personal and collective wisdom,
4. Nurturing the disposition, capacities, values, and skills of a servant-consciousness.

The *Practice* is useful for preparing for whatever an individual, or group, is about to do next. The practice is an efficient and effective way to physically ground and center oneself in preparation for any interior or exterior action, such as contemplation, physical exercise, a game, a hike, a presentation, a meeting, or a group process. Whether sitting in silence, standing, or walking, there is something very grounding about preparing for the *Practice* and then following through with each successive breath. Preparation for the practice involves internally imagining the body's vertical center and stating *I am here—now! I am here—now! I am now here!* We might also add the physical motion of moving the right hand up and down vertically aligning with the skeleton, which seems to initiate even more grounding and centering. Our physical body exists in the present and is perhaps our best conduit to awareness of the being in the present moment. There is a qualitative spatial difference from being present and being aware of our being present.

The *Practice* raises subtle awareness of greater interior depths, a deep affirming calm, and a sense of connectedness with all that is, and greater spatial awareness. Acknowledging and intentionally wishing the best for self and all our relations seems to create a relational framework for an ever but slowly growing capacity for inclusiveness that in turn affirms our relational responsibility. The *Practice*, while acknowledging our external relationships, also creates awareness and familiarity with responsibly holding space for others within our interior. Also, there seems to be a feeling of rightness when the cognitive mind attends to (serves) the rhythmic heart–mind; we may sense a warmhearted wholeness. Cognitively, we may experience a clearness and a sense of relaxed readiness, open to whatever is coming next.

Four Breath Presencing Practice is also an efficient conduit to presencing. Presencing is becoming present and available in our mind, heart, and our will in the immediacy of now. The *Practice* has proven quite helpful for preparing a group to journey through Scharmer's U methodology. It is especially helpful for preparing individuals and groups for empathetic and generative listening, generative dialog, and individual and group discernment. The more familiar a group is with the *Practice*, the quicker the collective comes to presencing, and often a more profound collective wisdom emerges as a result of the practice. *Four Breath Presencing Practice* can be a potent preparation for creative learning, aware healing, and transformational growth.

The *Practice* seems to help stimulate access to what Briskin, Erickson, Ott, and Callanan (2009) describe as the "unlimited cocreative power of groups..." (p. 147). In addition to presencing, a third interrelated purpose is using the *Practice* to prepare groups for their collective work. The *Practice* helps shift a group focusing primarily on cognitive knowing to include the rhythmic heart–mind fostering what McCraty, Bradly, and Tomasino (n.d.) referred to as psychophysiological coherence. After being guided through the *Practice*, a group is usually in a relational empathetic mode. The *Practice* helps raise awareness of our connectedness within ourselves and with others in the immediate group, and beyond. Accordingly, the *Practice* is useful for the U journey (Scharmer, 2009). The *Practice* affectively awakens and affirms a deep regard and sense of responsibility for our collective connectedness to each other and those in the greater world. This awareness enables groups to respectfully focus, and clarify their best intentions for those they serve, and creatively and generatively address whatever purpose lies before them. Using the *Practice* at the beginning of each gathering, such as at the beginning of a morning session, and again after lunch, helps group cohesion and focus. When an individual, a sub-group, or the entire group feels they are getting distracted or fragmented, the *Practice* can be done to help refocus.

The relational heart is naturally inclusive and holistic. Interestingly, due to the inherent relational aspect of this *Practice*, we never do this practice alone—even when we are alone. Relationally, the heart knows inclusivity the mind does not understand. It is like when we take a family picture, everyone wants to be included—the heart knows this. The heart does not want to leave anyone out. Experience using the practice reveals people previously not thought of may just come to mind during an inhale. Acceptance of these people is naturally inclusive and they become part of the practice from then on. Interestingly, when we hold a resentment toward someone, or we are projecting negativity toward a person or a situation, that awareness shows up immediately in the specific breath where that person/group is included (i.e., 3rd breath). It is like getting a speeding ticket; we get a relationship citation that we know needs to be addressed. This kind of internal mindful awareness is an example of the fruit of doing the practice regularly.

The *Practice* is profoundly relational and inherently inclusive. For example, individual and groups may shift between breath cycles—sometimes permanently, sometimes for a short period (depending on the situational context). After doing this practice for about a year, the insight occurred to me that my spouse and I (married 43 years at the time) were supposed to become *one* when we married. So I shifted her from *all those we love* (2nd breath) to *our oneness* (1st breath); there was an affirming rightness about doing that and she has remained there ever since. Since that time whenever and wherever someone shows up (regardless of the breath), they are freely included. Another example is when working with a group; after a couple of days, the group as a whole may shift from *those we are in relationship with* (3rd breath) into *those we love* (2nd breath), and they will remain in that breath for a period of time, perhaps a week or two, and then they shift back to the 3rd breath. Hence, no breath in the cycle is exclusive of others; each breath welcomes who ever shows up.

A fourth and longer term purpose of *Four Breath Presencing Practice* is to nurture a profoundly relational, creative, holistic, and integrative disposition. Servant-leaders in training gain experience and awareness of the profoundly relational *independence–interdependence* dynamic, a dynamic that when consciously engaged affirms the desire to serve-first. Acceptance of our greater relational responsibility affirms our awareness of the synergy of self-actualization and collective actualization. The *Practice* also affirms our internal awareness and a sense of responsibility to our relationship with our micro self and with others at the meso, macro, and mundo levels.

Sardello (2008) wrote of the importance of giving the mind a sacred task, to distract it from its self-absorption. The sacred task, the *Practice* evokes, begins by creating a very complex conundrum for the mind to imagine and actualize. The act of physically and imaginatively inhaling from all vertical and all horizontal directions into the heart corpus and then simultaneously exhaling in all directions is a multifaceted challenge for the imaginal mind. The task of engaging the mind on multiple levels of attention and intention, using the imagination, cognitive monitoring, thinking, feeling, recollecting, along with the awareness of the physical activity of actually doing each breath, is an exercise for our imaginal creative capacity.

Four Breath Presencing Practice is designed to nurture integrated wholeness. Speculatively, this is done by training the cognitive mind to become conscious of the relational nature of the rhythmic heart system, as well as the sensory capacity of the body system. Drawing the heart and body sensory systems into our conscious awareness is holistic integrative work. The *Practice* may also nurture emotional and moral intelligences. Our capacity for empathy extends to others, but also to ourselves, as does respect, forgiveness, and healing which positively affects our authenticity, integrity, and a grounded sense of humility. Serving-first reinforces all of this. When the cognitive mind is serving-first, the ego forgets about itself and attends to its primary relational function.

Finally, *Four Breath Presencing Practice* is designed to help us experientially sense, imagine, and integrate four worldviews (four stages of human development). Each breath symbolizes and parallels a stage of human development, affirming, expanding, and integrating Stages I and II and nurturing capacity for Stage III and Stage IV development. This occurs through the simultaneous stimulation of instrumental, imaginal, relational, and systems skills. The Practice can be used to stimulate awareness and build capacity to love all aspects of ourselves (Stage I), all family and relatives (Stage II), all others we are in relationship with (Stage III), and all of creation (Stage IV).

Four Breath Practice may help nurture our capacity for a Stage IV integrated holistic global worldview. As we enter Stage IV, we do so from primarily a Stage III frame of reference, but we also bring with us unintegrated fragments from Stages I and II. At Stage IV, one of the primary activities is the integration of all of the seemingly independent earlier stages. The *Practice* nurtures a sense of responsible awareness for our relationships and nurtures whole systems integration.

The *Four Breath Presencing Practice* is designed to stimulate a profoundly relational, creative, holistic, and integrative disposition (Fig. 7.2).

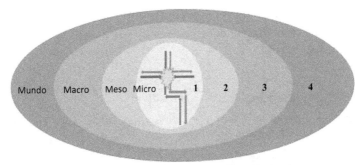

The Four Breath Presencing Practice

Centering on the Vertical and Horizontal Plane

Nurturing a servant-consciousness
Pause: Inhale: Pause: Exhale
In a pause identity and purpose may be changed.
A pause may change our world view, thus we change the world.

Fig. 7.2 Four breath presencing practice

- *Profoundly relational*: The practice nurtures a respectful, empathetic, personal, and collective awareness of our relational connectedness and evokes a moral responsibility for those relationships. The practice moves through micro, meso, macro to mundo, or ego-centrism, ethno-centrism, global-centrism, to cosmic-centrism.
- *Creative*: The practice stimulates our *imagining skills (imagining seven directions simultaneously)*. Imagining is essential for grounding and centering, for aware healing and creative learning, for moral development, for developing independence–interdependence, for holistic listening, for pathfinding-foresight, for systems thinking and stage development and worldview shifts. The pause before the inhale and the exhale is always symbolic and an actual opportune moment for aware healing and creative learning.
- *Holistic*: The practice mirrors the four stages of human development (I, I–You–It, I–You–It, I–We/It), acknowledges the internal and external as one, and engages the physical, sensory and feeling, cognitive, and spiritual (body, heart, mind, will).
- *Integrative*: The Practice is all inclusive and exponentially expanding; nothing is intentionally lost in the continuous centering and clarifying

of the interior with the exterior. The four stages of development become a differentiated oneness, especially when a wisdom structure is consciously accessed.

Four Breath Presencing Practice (*Narrative*)

Preparation: Ground and Center yourself. When ready: Say *I am here—now! I am here—now! I am now here!*

(Our First Breath is for our Oneness)
Pause: Inhale from all directions, all the Blessings and Grace we are in most need of for the well-being of our oneness (physical, emotional, cognitive, & spiritual).
Pause: Exhale healing and blessings in all directions, through every sphere of our oneness.

(Our Second Breath is for all those we love)
Pause: Inhale from all directions, all the Blessings and Grace we are in most need of for the well-being of our oneness; and for all whom we love *(spouse, children, grandchildren, siblings and their families, mother, father, grandmothers, grandfathers, all our marital & blood relations.)*
Pause: Exhale healing and blessings in all directions, to all those whom we love and serve.

(Our Third Breath is for the wellbeing of all our known relationships)
Pause: Inhale from all directions, all the Blessings and Grace we are in most need of for the wellbeing of our oneness; for all whom we love; and all those we are in relationship with; those we know and have known, all those we interact with, even those we might not care for; all individuals and groups; especially those who come to mind now *(some individuals, groups, may come to mind).*
Pause: Exhale healing and blessings in all directions, to all whom we know and serve.

(Our Fourth Breath is for the wellbeing of all that is)
Pause: Inhale from all directions, all the Blessings and Grace we are in most need of for the wellbeing of our oneness; for all whom we love; all whom we are in relationship with; and all that is; all people, especially those who suffer, even those who may wish to harm us, those who have passed and those yet to be; all animals; all living things, the entire earth, and beyond—to the mystery of all that *is* and *is not*.
Pause: Exhale healing and blessings in all directions to all that we serve—the known and unknown.

Pause: momentarily notice and be with the feeling of connectedness with all our relations.

Summation

I believe the world is in great need of leadership studies that strive to hold to the classic values, virtues, and wisdom of humanity while nurturing a transforming vision of humanities greatness. As the world becomes progressively more complex, diversified, and fragmented in this era, it is very important to clarify leader and collective human values that create human flourishing on a global and even a cosmic scale. As our global societies move more and more into a multi-generational workforce and probe further into the universe. We need to view the workforce developmentally and with compassionate understanding. We need to embrace the reality that the majority of the workforce will likely always be in Stage I and Stage II developmentally, and we need to embrace them where they are at and create systems and programs that call them forth into Stage III and eventually into Stage IV development.

The focus of this book has been on Stage III and Stage IV development. The primary focus of Servant-leader development at Stage III is value clarity, and the core capacities for developing clarity are holistic listening and pathfinding-foresight. These two capacities synergistically enrich the rightness of adhering to moral principles and promoting communities that nurture self-actualization and collective actualization, and further nurture the systems thinking and the personal development of a global systems worldview. All of which supports the formation of a Stage IV worldview and an emerging servant-consciousness.

References

Anonymous. (2002). *Meditations on the Tarot: A journey into Christian Hermeticism*. (R. Powell Trans. New York: Jeremy P. Tarcher / Putnam.

Briskin, A., Erickson, S., Ott, J., & Callanan, T. (2009). *The power of collective wisdom: And the trap of collective folly*. San Francisco: Barrett-Koehler.

Campbell, J. (1986). *The inner reaches of outer space: Metaphor as myth and as religion*. New York: Perennial Library.

Catholic Encyclopedia. *Humility*. Retrieved January 11, 2018., from http://www.catholic.org/encyclopedia/view.php?id=5969

Delman, R. (2018). *Personal communication*. Sebatopol, CA: The Embodied Life School.

Hall, B. P. (1994). *Values shift: A guide to personal & organizational transformation*. Rockport, MA: Twin Lights.

Kirkley, J. (2009). *Humility*. Retrieved February 9, 2010, from http://revkirkley.blogspot.com/2009/01/longish-post-on-purity-of-heart.html

McCraty, R. Bradly R. T., & Tomasino, D. (n.d.). *The heart has its own brain and consciousness*. Retrieved November 2016 from http://in5d.com/the-heart-has-its-own-brain-and-consciousness/

Sardello, R. (2008). *Silence: The mystery of wholeness*. Benson, NC: Golden Stone Press.

Scharmer, O. (2009). *Theory U: Leading from the future as it emerges*. San Francisco: Berrett-Koehler.

Sparough, J. M., Manney, J., & Hipskind, T. (2010). *What's your decision? How to make choices with confidence and clarity: An Ignatian approach to decision making*. Chicago, IL: Loyola Press.

Index

© The Author(s) 2018
J. H. Horsman, *Servant-Leaders in Training*,
Palgrave Studies in Workplace Spirituality and Fulfillment,
https://doi.org/10.1007/978-3-319-92961-3

Collective(s) (*cont.*)
   156, 157, 167–169, 171,
   173–178, 182, 185, 187
 development, 4, 5, 14, 34, 100
 wisdom, 86, 115, 125, 147, 151,
   158, 159, 169, 170, 181, 182
Come to know, 116, 166
Commitment, 9, 12, 44, 49, 82, 91,
   92, 99, 103, 104, 109, 122,
   123, 131, 144, 150, 162, 163,
   165, 166
Communitarian, 41, 49, 55, 56, 60,
   61, 65, 73
Community, xix, 1, 9–13, 15, 19, 26,
   28, 43, 46, 52–54, 59, 61,
   71–75, 77, 80, 82, 86, 96–102,
   108, 109, 113, 141, 158,
   162–165, 174, 175, 178, 187
Compassion, 4, 13, 20–23, 61, 71,
   74, 79, 83, 92–94, 96, 98,
   103, 108, 122, 127, 131, 150,
   163, 167
Conceptualization/conceptualizes,
   xii, 9, 11, 19, 39, 72, 73,
   80–82, 89, 90, 123–126, 140,
   143, 147, 153, 154, 159
Confidence, 15, 72, 106
Congruence/congruent, 12, 50, 53,
   55, 56, 73, 86, 90, 95,
   105–108, 127, 132, 133, 176
Congruent harmony, 106
Create/creating/creation, 3, 11, 18,
   20, 25, 51–53, 55, 56, 62, 64,
   75, 82, 85, 89, 91–93, 96, 97,
   101, 106, 120, 124–126, 133,
   134, 141, 151–153, 156, 157,
   159, 162–164, 168–170, 176,
   181, 183, 184, 187

Creative learning, xiii, 13, 23, 27,
   55, 77, 85, 97, 98, 114, 115,
   125, 126, 131, 133, 137,
   143–152, 155, 159, 182, 185
Creativity, xiii, 50, 52, 54, 56, 60,
   67, 68, 77, 104, 108, 109,
   124, 126, 136, 151–154, 177
Culture, 2, 4, 26, 54, 65, 69, 70, 82,
   85, 93, 98, 100, 103, 113,
   116, 132, 169, 173, 174

D

Dependable, 108, 109
Development, xiii, 2–7, 9–17, 24,
   29, 33–43, 49, 50, 52, 54–57,
   59–86, 92–95, 100–103, 109,
   115, 120, 134, 137, 145, 146,
   148, 152, 155, 156, 159, 161,
   168, 173, 174, 180, 184–187
Dialog, 99, 125, 126, 131–133, 149
Dignity, 18, 28, 49, 51, 54, 79, 83,
   95, 116, 130, 165
Discerning, 83, 91, 93, 127, 129, 130,
   141, 142, 147, 148, 167, 170
Discernment, xiii, 91, 108, 116,
   122, 127–129, 170, 182

E

Ecological, 1, 53, 84, 107, 171
Eco-system, 28, 38, 54, 63, 65, 79,
   107, 156, 171
Ego, 24, 25, 27, 41, 134, 165–167,
   184, 185
Emerge, xi, 4, 16–20, 25, 28, 33, 37,
   39, 47, 49, 55, 56, 60, 61, 69,
   91, 92, 97, 114–116, 121,

CPSIA information can be obtained
at www.ICGtesting.com
Printed in the USA
LVHW051736180419
614692LV00009B/270/P